Spiritual Pragmatism

A Practical Approach to Spirit Work in a World Controlled by Ego

By

Endall Beall

First Edition

Copyright © 2015 Endall Beall
All Rights Reserved
ISBN-13: 978-1517313258
ISBN-10: 1517313252

Dedication

This book is dedicated to those individuals who possess the inner strength and courage to alter the path of human consciousness for the betterment of all humanity by altering themselves.

Table of Contents

ACKNOWLEDGEMENTS
Foreword xi
Introduction 14
1. The Tyranny of Mind Control 20
2. The Challenging Ego 34
3. A World Without Accountability 49
4. Presumed Authority 63
5. The Band-Aid Solutions... 77
6. Fabian Gradualism and Hegelian Dialectic 92
7. The Other Side of the Coin...114
8. The Robber Barons 123
9. Fabian Socialism and New Age Indoctrination.................135
10. The Prime Example 146
Afterword 156

ACKNOWLEDGEMENTS

I would like to acknowledge my dear friend Phil who generously allowed me to use his artwork to grace the cover of this book.

I would also like to acknowledge all the historical researchers whose efforts over the years have worked to unravel the maze of public historical deception and help shine the light of truth on this historical chicanery.

Foreword

The book you hold is your hand is the foundation for a much needed dialogue that has to take place where the advancement of human cognition is concerned. That dialogue is about spiritual pragmatism. After decades of personal study, the one thing I found keenly lacking in every teaching about spirituality, whether it is religious spirituality or mystical spirituality, is a sense of spiritual pragmatism.

Every avenue of modern spiritual understanding, no matter how it is marketed to the public at large, eventually devolves into some sort of mystical or supernatural interpretations about spirit and what people *think* spirit is or should be. At its base element, spirit is nothing more than one's own higher level consciousness which, in its natural state, is not bound by matter or the material form. When I refer to spirit, or the spirit self throughout every book I have written, I am speaking about the higher level immaterial consciousness that currently serves as the animating force behind your human form, what some researchers into consciousness refer to as 'mind'.

Through the aegis of thousands of years of indoctrination, first by people who had a specific agenda to keep human consciousness restrained and controlled, then through multitudes of generations of humans who lacked any clear understanding of the principles or nature of spirit, spirit has been defined as either a soul that needs salvation, a part of your soul that somehow needs to connect or reconnect to God, or a fragment of consciousness that ultimately needs to connect back to some overarching consciousness of which the human mind is simply a minor offshoot, and which, if we can reconnect to this overarching consciousness, will ultimately provide all the answers we seek where spiritual understanding is concerned. Every one of these concepts is in error. Everyone of these concepts promote some idea about spiritual dependency, and as such, these ideas have left humans ever-searching but never finding the solutions about what spirit actually is.

Every concept of spirit on this planet is threaded through a needle of dependency. These mistaken concepts all set humans at a cognitive disadvantage by teaching reliance on some enigmatic outside force to do for us what each of us has the capability to do for ourselves without the dependency syndrome of modern and ancient spiritual traditions, no matter how they are packaged to sell to their respective audiences. This book is about opening a dialogue on spiritual self-reliance and spiritual pragmatism that is greatly needed for the human species on this planet at this time if we are ever to evolve past the problems that currently infect our consciousness and are the basis for every ill we find in the world today.

I went to great lengths to emphasize the need for spiritual pragmatism in my book *Demystifying the Mystical,* and this book is going to focus more fully on what spiritual pragmatism is and how we can change the world for the better, if we can only find the willingness to change ourselves and our present mode of cognitive operation. What I propose in this book is not impossible to do, but it also not easy for anyone to achieve. It is one thing to scream about the problems of the world and become aware of them, but it takes more to provide actual workable solutions to these problems than it does to merely point them out. This book is not going to provide a solution to every problem that ails humanity at this time, but it is designed to highlight some of the problems that can be addressed through more public awareness of their existence without getting on the gloom and doom pulpit of rabid conspiracy theorists and those who preach helplessness and fear in the face of these problems. We are not helpless. *You* are not helpless in the face of this seeming cognitive juggernaut. The only helpless people are those who continue to believe they are helpless.

Introduction

This book is about spiritual pragmatism. The only way it can be written is through exposing the impracticality of the majority of current systems of spiritual beliefs, whether they be mystical or religious. This book is written for those who have tired of the unpragmatic interpretations about what true spirituality actually is and the mystical framework that is peddled as spiritual truths in so many philosophical and mystical schools of thought.

To those who may still be wrapped up in these unpragmatic belief systems, this book is going to be perceived as nothing more than someone taking potshots at their belief structure. What every reader has to realize is that I *am* taking potshots at these systems of belief, but that I *am not* taking potshots at them personally for accepting such beliefs. A person can change their beliefs by a simple choice when they have enough information to show that the belief is not what it presents itself to be. A belief *system* is already in place and will not change, it can only be set aside for more practical truths.

All belief systems are simply inanimate ideas that people attach themselves to because they make the ego part of themselves feel that they belong to a group, a religion, a political party or a culture. The *belief system* itself has no conscious awareness, it has no identity and it has no feelings that can be hurt. Beliefs are simply ideas that our egos give life to in the hope that the ego self can fit in with other egos who have the same need of dependency on one belief system or another.

Behind every belief structure there is an originator. Once a belief structure gains adherents, this belief structure begins to take on a life of its own as individuals who agree with the belief program start to flex power through their gathered followers. When you add money to this crowd of devoted believers putting forward their belief structure, you can manipulate the world. There is a major hidden agenda in the modern spiritual movement in the west that goes beyond the notice of those who are seeking fluffy escapist ideas about what seekers *think* spiritual pursuits are *supposed* to represent. These followers are buying into an illusory system of beliefs which has been highly managed and manipulated for well over 100 years. This book provides an introduction to this manipulation and some of the organizations responsible for framing the doctrines in the modern spiritual movement.

In the vast majority of cases, humans are driven by the ego program, no matter how much their ego consciousness wants to rebel at that idea. The ego program is highly adaptable and can change its beliefs whenever it feels a need to follow any belief that makes the ego feel good about itself, makes it feel that it is 'on the right track', or that fulfills any sense of the ego's need for acceptance. In that regard, the ego program is hopelessly dependent on outside belief structures to validate itself, as well as a reliance on others who share that belief to reinforce one's own choice to believe it at all. The more people who accept any particular system of belief, the more the ego can grow comfortable and become part of a group ego mentality.

When it gets right down to it, the ego will believe anything that makes it feel psychologically comfortable. When one becomes psychologically comfortable with any belief system, the ego then serves as a defender of this belief system, whatever it may be, for the ego self-identity then embraces the belief as part of itself. The outcome of this is that if anyone challenges the belief system, the ego perceives the challenge as a direct assault against itself, turns defensive, and refuses to acknowledge any truth that may threaten that belief. The distinction between the ego program and the belief structure is no longer differentiated and they become one and the same. It is rare indeed to find an individual who can discuss their beliefs objectively without the need to defend them.

As noted by the psychologist Leon Festinger in his *Theory of Cognitive Dissonance*, the personality of the individual (let's be specific and call that the ego personality), will do everything in its power to avoid a state of cognitive dissonance. (Cognitive dissonance occurs when someone finds their belief system to be false, or their perception of reality is challenged so severely that a form of psychological discomfort occurs - i.e. cognitive dissonance.) The ego program in everyone will go to any extreme in order to argue away the truth and maintain its beliefs and retain what Festinger called cognitive consonance, whereby the ego personality will do everything at its disposal to rationalize away any truth that undermines its own belief structure.

The constant pursuit of the ego to maintain its own internal sense of perceptual consonance is what leads to so many irrational beliefs in the realm of spiritual pursuits. The blind faith in any belief system also creates a form of willful denial of things that point out that the belief may not be what it seems. The ego program, once it accepts its own individual belief system, becomes not simply a believer of the system, but also a staunch defender of the system.

The more one challenges an ego's belief system, the more the ego digs in its heels to maintain and defend the belief, rather than admit it could remotely be *wrong*. A challenge to the belief is perceived as a direct assault on the ego personality itself. This defensiveness is more pronounced in the pursuits of spirituality and religion than anywhere else in the human psyche, although these are not the only types of beliefs that can dominate the ego. Once one adopts the belief in any type of mystical or supernatural solution where understanding spirit is concerned, they have already so handicapped their consciousness through their own ego's dependency on the belief, that one can rarely tell them the truth without winding up on the receiving end of vitriolic verbal defensiveness.

This book is going to expose a very dark agenda hiding behind the modern spiritual movement. This book contains facts that are easily verifiable if one chooses to seek them out. These facts are going to make some people very uncomfortable because they are going to disrupt perceptions about so-called spirituality that many are going to be unwilling to face, and will vehemently deny.

Within these pages I am going to challenge many different areas of belief, particularly the spiritual belief systems that teach docility and seeking a perpetual life of mystical spiritual peace. Few who are seeking spirit have not fallen prey to a certain level of hidden political indoctrination, which is going to be the primary focus of this book. The New Age system of spiritual pursuits is not what it appears to be on its face, and there is a hidden political agenda behind it that is manipulating people's minds into a state of cognitive complacency designed to fulfill a larger and much darker political agenda.

I am going to offer historically verifiable information that everyone on the spirit path needs to be made aware of if they ever expect to gain any sense of spiritual pragmatism. True spiritual pragmatism is found when one can accept total responsibility for their own consciousness, and that can't be achieved so long as we relinquish that responsibility to ourselves when we blindly accept things because it makes our ego feel good about itself.

We live in a world with a lot of real, hard problems. Some of those problems are explored in this book, as well as some potential solutions. The main focus of this material is to lift people out of beliefs that leave them willfully ignorant and complacent about what is happening in the world around us. This complacent attitude is especially prevalent in the modern spiritual community, and it is that community that needs to recognize that the ideas about escapist spirituality are not going to change the world for the better.

If you don't have the courage within you to face the idea that your beliefs may be totally incorrect from the standpoint of someone challenging an unthinking and unfeeling belief system, and you choose to continue to use your belief system as a form of ego self-identity, then you are invited to put this book down because chances are that your ego is going to force you to deny the truth presented anyway. If, on the other hand, you are one of those who is tired of the circus of violence, ignorance and tyranny that has been ever present on this planet since the human species was created, and who is a person genuinely looking for real solutions rather than Band-Aid solutions that never work, then please, read on.

1. The Tyranny of Mind Control

To start this chapter, let's look at the definition of what mind control is. The following definition can be found on Wikipedia under Mind Control:

> "Mind control (also known as brainwashing, reeducation, coercive persuasion, thought **control,** or thought reform) is a theoretical indoctrination process which results in "an impairment of autonomy, inability to think independently, and a disruption of beliefs and affiliations."

The first thing that must be acknowledged if we ever expect to advance ourselves cognitively as a species is the fact that our entire perceptual reality has come about through a form of multigenerational brainwashing - a form of cultural mind control. This is not theoretical, it is an actuality for every human being on this planet. Because everyone finds themselves subject to this indoctrinational brainwashing, they rarely see it for what it is, because everyone else is subject to it as well. Every aspect of mind control originates from external sources through our parents, peer groups, religious groups or a cultural group exercising its own form of indoctrination to shape their children to conform within all of these (and other) accepted 'norms'. For untold generations of human beings on this planet, we have been told what reality is and what it is not, and if we do not happen to agree with this indoctrinated perception of reality, we have an army of psychologists and psychiatrists who can either psychoanalyze or drug us back into compliance with the accepted cultural norms. There is not one single individual on this planet to date who has not suffered at the hands of this type of multigenerational cultural brainwashing. It is nothing but a form of self-enforced species mind control passed on by one generation of controlling egos to the next generation to create more controlled egos.

Once the boundaries of 'reality' have been hammered into us long enough, when we are finally so indoctrinated that we start to fit into our culturally-defined reality, then we are confronted with the various peer groups and multitudes of belief systems into which our now-indoctrinated egos can traverse, so long as they don't make waves and become a real disruption to this defined 'reality'. As long as you are not hurting anyone else, it seems, one is allowed to believe all the ludicrous nonsense they care to embrace. I ask the reader to show me anywhere in such a system of perceptual reality where they can find an ounce of pragmatism. So, lets take a look at the definition of what being pragmatic is:

> *"Pragmatic - (adjective) - dealing with things sensibly and realistically in a way that is based on practical rather than theoretical considerations."*

Now, let's take a look at the word practical, since practicality is the basis of pragmatism:

> *"Practical - (adjective) - Relating to what is real rather than what is possible or imagined.*
> *Likely to succeed and reasonable to do or use.*
> *Appropriate or suited for actual use.*

When we read these definitions, we find that pragmatism has to do with relating to what is real versus what is merely theoretical. All of humanity has been indoctrinated with a hardline definition of cognitive reality through multiple generations of people programming the next generation with the same perceptual definition of reality they were indoctrinated with, whether that definition is right or wrong. Every human has had these boundaries of reality indoctrinated into them for so many generations that no one bothers to question whether the boundaries of current perceptions of reality are correct or not.

We just accept it because everyone else does and no one knows any real difference or seems willing to investigate it.

Where this boundary of defined reality is stretched to its limits is where mysticism and beliefs in the supernatural are concerned, for it is here that the grasp of defined reality becomes more tenuous. The other end of this spectrum lies in the stark dependency on harsh rationalism and the scientific method and the denial of anything that can't be measured and quantified through current material experimentation within these defined boundaries of material reality. Between these two extremes lays the understanding of the spirit self, or the second cognition.

As we have explained throughout *The Evolution of Consciousness* series of books that spirit is simply a word, a *definition* of a concept that is not generally understood when one is operating fully in the first cognition realm of thinking. Consciousness is the source of everything in the material world. The consciousness begotten by the ego program is but a pale shadow of higher level consciousness found when one can advance into a higher state of cognitive awareness that I call the second cognition, which can only be tuned into when one can supersede the ego and all of its programming. This higher state of perceptual awareness is available to every human being on the planet that wishes to access it, provided they are willing to do the necessary work to achieve it for themselves. In this regard, reaching the second cognition is practical because its effects can be repeated through different individuals working to achieve the same tangible goal. It is not theoretical and, as such, it is therefore very pragmatic.

The first set of myths we have to explode is that spirit is some sort of supernatural part of us, that it is somehow separated from us, and that through some kind of religious belief system or through mystical practices, we can somehow supernaturally ultimately 'reconnect' with it. Not a single human being on this planet is remotely disconnected from their own spirit, for it is only a higher level of conscious awareness that lies buried under generations of indoctrinational programming that the ego program in all of us has adopted as its own particular brand of reality. When we can recognize such ego dependencies for what they are and get rid of our reliance on such beliefs and the requirement for supernatural explanations to define spirit, then we can each start peeling back the layers of ego indoctrination that keep us harnessed within this limited perception of reality. Until we, as a species, can undo this ego program and its indoctrinational programming, then humanity as a whole will be continually bound in a world of seemingly insurmountable problems and very few real solutions, for it is the ego program itself that lies at the root of all the world's problems and is, unfortunately, also in charge of providing any solutions to the problems it creates.

The individual ego embraces whatever belief systems it desires in order to make itself feel good, feel accepted and maintain a form of psychological consonance with itself. It doesn't matter to the ego program which variety of beliefs it accepts to define its own reality so long as the ego is satisfied with itself that it has made the most rewarding choices to gratify its own psychologically selfish desires. Where most modern and ancient spiritual pursuits find their greatest appeal is through ideas about supernatural interventions in one form or another.

•Many of the mystical and religious belief systems are heavily dependent on some form of supernatural salvation or some type of spiritual escapism that is going to magically remove people from this world and mystically progress them into either a heavenly afterlife or some state of spiritual reward that alleviates their psyche from the responsibilities of dealing with the world around them. Advancing into the second cognition will provide none of these escapist scenarios. If anything, it makes people more realistic and pragmatic in accepting their responsibility when they realize that all of these escapist scenarios are exactly that, a relinquishment and avoidance of personal responsibility. There is nothing pragmatic about that type of spirituality. Nothing whatsoever.

One of the primary misconceptions of mystical beliefs is about so-called enlightenment. Too many people seem to expect enlightenment to bring them some kind of release from their earthly responsibilities. Enlightenment, as Buddha described it, amounted to nothing more than him conquering his own ego, through his own form of coming to terms with the disruption in his own life, and dealing with the cognitive dissonance that was a result of that disruption. This life disruption is what caused Buddha to start his own process of ego self-analysis that eventually led to him surpassing his own ego and moving into the second cognition. There is nothing mystical either with the process or the higher level of consciousness he attained as a result of this. I explained the meaning of the nine virtues of Buddha in chapter 2 of my book, *Recovering Spirit After the 2012 Disappointment.* Nowhere in those explanations will anyone find a whiff of mysticism or religion in explaining their meaning.

As I have explained in pieces throughout *The Evolution of Consciousness* series, where the avenue of mysticism arose in Buddhism is when people operating in the first cognition came behind Buddha and turned what he taught into a form of mystical misdirection. The Hindu priesthood of that era wasted no time after Buddha's death in establishing the system of mystical monasticism, which Buddha did not initiate during his lifetime, and it is this Hindu-cum-Buddhist system of mysticism that is sold as institutionalized Buddhism today. Institutional Buddhism has elevated Buddha to the state of a near-deity and has totally corrupted his teachings about the second cognition. This *always* happens when first cognition egos get control of second cognition concepts that they do not remotely comprehend, and therefore attach mystical explanations to the process because they lack the cognitive awareness to correctly interpret the concept.

Five to six hundred years after Buddha, a Hebrew man named Immanuel taught the same principles of the second cognition, and when first cognition egos got hold of his ideas, they deified him, renamed him Jesus, and Christianity was born as another mystical religious system of mind control that teaches people to always look outside themselves and rely on Jesus to fix their lives for them. Along with this concept, (Christianity removed the responsibility from people for taking care of this world and sold them the concept of the afterlife. The believers got so concerned about their rewards in the afterlife that they forsook all responsibilities for taking care of this world except converting others to their mystical doctrine or die. The biblical provision to subdue the Earth is what has led us to the exploitation of the planet into modern times. To this day, every Christian has their eyes and minds so focused on the mystical return of Jesus and their happy hereafter, or their dread of Satan, that they relinquish their responsibility to make this world a better place for everyone.)

Every religion on this planet teaches the same type of dependency on some god or another, the pursuit after some mystical sense of oneness that we have all been separated from, or reaching a state of enlightenment that removes the burden of our earthly responsibilities from ourselves. This sense of mystical dependency plays right into the hands of the ego personality which has been indoctrinated worldwide with the dependence on external authority. In the case of religions, they all teach the perceptual reliance on the greatest authority of all - either a God or gods, or the grand cosmic oneness. It is a dependency syndrome of the worst kind predicated on untold generations of blind acceptance of external authority, regardless of whom or what that authority might be.

You may initially want to balk at this claim that humans have a profound tendency to obey authority, but there was a controversial study done in the 1960's by Stanley Milgram into why people in Nazi Germany would blindly follow orders leading to torture and death and resulting in the Holocaust. In this study, Milgram set up a series of tests where a test subject was hired to issue electric shocks to another person who was, unknown to the research subject, a part of the research team. The basis of the study was to see whether people would balk at issuing ever-elevating levels of electric shock to their 'learner' if they failed to provide correct answers to a word-matching questionnaire. The device that delivered the shocks to the learner was set to deliver the shocks that started at 15 volts and went up to 450 volts, with two additional levels above the 450 volts simply marked XXX.

The study was designed to see whether the subject of the study, operating under the instructions and guidance of an authority figure, in this case the researcher himself, would stop issuing electric shocks to the 'learner' in the experiment when they got too painful, or whether they would continue to induce pain to an unknown innocent victim at the direction of the authority figure of the researcher. Without going into all the permutations of the experiment, in the majority of cases, the test subjects blindly obeyed the commands of the researcher authority figure, despite the subjects often voicing their own misgivings about continuing the experiments when the 'learner' complained of pain or couldn't answer the questions. The case study can be found in Milgram's book *Obedience to Authority*. For informational purposes, the 'learner' in the experiment never received any shocks, but was an actor hired by the researcher to scream out in pain and protest as the test continued and the presumed levels of electric shock were elevated. No one was physically harmed in the experiment, despite what the test subjects issuing the electric jolts thought throughout the experiment.

    The point I'm working to establish here is that humans operating under ego will do many things so long as their ego psyche can rationalize why they would do such things, and in most cases, it amounted to the test subjects rationalizing the fact that the authority figure was presumed to know more about things than they themselves did, and was therefore responsible for their actions, not themselves. Based on this presumption of authoritative superiority, many test subjects rationalized away their actions by deferring to a presumed representative of higher authority than take responsibility for their own actions. In other words, "I was just following orders".

Many psychological studies seek to find the basis of why people act and react the way they do. What each and every one of these psychological researchers has failed to take into consideration is the root of the problem, which is the ego program itself. The ego program is so embedded and accepted as a part of the human psyche that these researchers are all so bold as to call this 'human nature', without having an ounce of understanding about what the underlying cause of this behavior is. It is not human nature, it is *ego nature*. Every one of these researchers is as deeply infected with the ego program as everyone else and they can't see the forest for the trees. The actions of their own egos, as presumed authority figures, blinds them to this reality. They can't see it so they never bring it into their psychological studies as a factor of their research. It is the one major factor that is continually overlooked in their psychological experimental evaluations.

Human beings on this planet have never, since they were created, been allowed any type of true freedom of consciousness. We were made as slaves to the so-called gods, those who tampered with our genetics in a laboratory and produced this species about 200,000 years ago. As a result of being produced as a race of slaves, humanity on this planet had the *obedience to authority syndrome* drilled into them from the start. Human consciousness has no understanding of real freedom of consciousness without the institutions of authority and obedience to all the different levels of hierarchal authority that govern every society on the planet today. This obedience to authority, starting with the inception of the human race on this planet, has become the model of our ego-oriented societies. This deference to authority started with the offworlders who eventually called themselves gods. They were the ultimate authorities, and in every religion on the planet today, the authority of god is always cited as the basis for religious wars and indoctrination through conversion to the varied faiths.

From the gods this system of authority was passed down through their earthly intercessors and agents, the priests. From priestly hierarchies, humans continued the tradition of requiring authority through secular means with the invention of kingship. Naturally, kings and queens needed their 'advisors', and with this need of advisors we see the spawning of bureaucracies and the hierarchies of the petty bureaucratic tyrants all over the world, all modeled, of course, on priestly hierarchies. Since academia was established by the university system created by the Catholic Church, this academic endeavor developed its own form of hierarchal control called the peer review system.

It doesn't matter where we turn in any society on this planet, from the roughest tribal community living isolated in some deep jungle to the most esteemed institutions on the planet, humans all defer to this authoritative control in one form or another. The path to success under the present system of ego control is to become an authority yourself and thereby have the capability to lord it over others who are not as fortunate enough to climb the ladder of authority. At the root of all of this one finds the ego personality. If psychologists want to understand why people more often blindly obey authority than not, then they have to understand the underlying cause, and that cause is the dependency of the ego on outside sources to validate everything it thinks or believes. If god isn't the authority, it is governmental authority or peer reviewed authority, but in all cases it amounts to seeking external authoritative answers that validates what every ego chooses to believe, and also validates the ego's very existence.

Any experiment that starts on a false foundation is going to deliver faulty results. Milgram's study into obedience left the researchers puzzled as to the results attained from the study. They varied the components of the study to test whether people would react the same if peers were issuing the instructions versus the authority figure, and the results gathered from this variation of the study showed that people would challenge an average person and stop the experiment, whereas under the direction of an authority figure, they would continue delivering higher level doses of electric shock to the learner in the experiments. They reviewed certain subjects in the book after the fact and offered their psychological prognostications on why certain subjects psychologically rationalized their actions, but with absolutely no understanding of the ego program itself, the results of the experiment left the researchers with the data that proved a tendency for humans to bow to authority without ultimately discovering why this was so. Without factoring in the workings of the ego program, which I covered extensively in *Demystifying the Mystical,* the researchers could not arrive at the root-cause of the psychology behind the actions of the test subjects in the experiments.

Milgram's study was performed by Yale university, which gave the experiment another air of authoritative legitimacy to the test subjects due to the presumed authority and notoriety of the institution itself. The fact is that any huckster could have made the same claim and most people would not question the authority behind such experimentation, especially if they were being paid to participate. It is this presumption of authority that leaves the ego personality open to all sorts of abuse, not just by outsiders, but abuse by the ego program itself on our individual consciousness. This foundation has to be established in order to understand why people embrace so many beliefs, whether they are spiritual or scientific. Until we can understand the underlying root of this need for external authority, then we can't understand what drives the ego system of the first cognition that rules the consciousness of virtually every human being on this planet at this point in human history.

2. The Challenging Ego

What I found astounding over the years progressing through my own development in cognitive advancement is how utterly jealous the ego program is when it comes to authority. The ego program will readily embrace someone as a spiritual authority who dresses as a Yogi and spews out all sorts of mystical nonsense rather than give in to the idea that anyone else of equal stature as themselves can achieve enlightenment on their own. The ego will readily embrace any belief that appeals to its own sense of self-gratification in this world, no matter how ludicrous that belief might be, so long as its source presents itself to be some kind of authority. Books like *The Secret* have sold millions of copies worldwide, masquerading as hidden spiritual principles of some alleged Law of Attraction, yet when one looks at the material provided in *The Secret* and others like it, they find ideas that cater strictly to the ego's sense of greed wrapped in presumed mystical doctrines.

The Secret plays on the most base of human ego instincts, the desire for more money, a better job, or finding love. These are all needs of the ego self and founded in crass material desires, and just because the authors have made millions of dollars by producing seminars and getting star endorsements by peddling their own Law of Attraction mystical pap, the unwitting egos who buy into these books and pay to attend the seminars looking for some magical solution to their lives are only deceiving themselves. They are not moving one inch closer to understanding the spirit self, but are instead chasing materialistic rainbows wrapped in mystical swill. There is nothing spiritually pragmatic about pursuing such avenues of alleged spirituality, regardless of how it is marketed to the unsuspecting, spiritually-hungry egos who so willingly buy into it seeking their own individual forms of mystical ego gratification.

What the producers of *The Secret* never tell you is the alleged hidden source of all these secret teachings and, unfortunately, few egos have the temerity to even ask about where the teachings originated. They just accept this quasi-spiritual bullshit blindly, expecting magical manifestations in wealth, love and a better lifestyle. Their egos are so hungry for that material gratification that they are willing to buy this stuff in order to fulfill their ego's selfish material desires, and if it is wrapped in an air of mystical mystery, then the greater the fascination it holds for the ego looking for easy solutions. The writers of the book are fully aware of how easy it is to entice someone into their bogus belief systems through offering magical material gains. The authors of the book don't bother to tell the greedy egos that flock to their seminars that the Law of

Attraction has its origins in the Theosophical teachings of Madame Helena Blavatsky, which I covered at length in my book *Operator's Manual for the True Spirit Warrior*.

Theosophy is the hidden agenda behind the modern New Age, and there is a very powerful political reason behind its adaptations over the last century and a quarter. Theosophy is allegedly the mystical and political answer to the tyranny of Christianity, and it is simply one mystical belief system competing with another mystical belief system called religion. There is not one aspect of the modern New Age that can't trace its origins back to Madame Blavatsky's and Alice Bailey's brands of Theosophy.

Theosophy is like a snowball that is pushed from the top of a mountain. As it progresses down the hill, it gathers up everything in its path as it increases in size, but at the core we still find that original snowball that started the ball rolling. Since Blavatsky created Theosophy, which is a combination of ancient occult mysticism, Hinduism and certain principles of Buddhism mixed with mystical Christianity and Islam, the Theosophy snowball has gathered in the material from the I AM movement, neo-Gnosticism, Wicca, neo-Paganism, Freemasonry, and folded in the aliens, ever since the Roswell incident happened in 1947.

The modern so-called spiritual movements, whether they be the New Age, Wicca or the esoteric doctrines of Aliester Crowley and neo-Paganism, each and every one, teach and preach some sort of dependency on supernaturalism or mysticism as their core principles. It seems that all anyone has to do the make money in this arena is claim to be enlightened, fill their written works with enough mystical riddles to sound 'spiritual', and they are now qualified to bilk millions of people out of their hard earned money to sit at the feet of these self-proclaimed gurus. Not a one of these alleged authorities can teach you anything of true spiritual value because they are simply part of the authoritative spiritual indoctrination machine. Not a one of them can tell you how to achieve their mystical state of enlightenment for one very simple reason, they are not enlightened at all. They are only selling a mystical product based on a script that is thousands of years old.

At the outset I want to pose a question to the reader about levitation. Within the New Age arena you find a fascination with levitation and how it is supposed to equate to mystical enlightenment. I ask the reader this, when it comes to advancing your cognitive capabilities, what kind of importance is there in being able to levitate? Do you honestly think that performing some kind of magical parlor trick is really going to move you an inch forward in your own cognitive advancement?

I am going to point the reader to a video on Youtube wherein some Yogi is allegedly teaching people how to levitate. Watch the video *Art of Levitation Unleashed by Nithyananda* and you will see a bunch of people using a yogic technique to jump into the air a few inches. This, purportedly, is how one learns to levitate. It is curious, however, that this grand Yogi teaching this bullshit can give no example whatsoever of his own presumed ability to levitate by doing so himself, because it can't be done. It is simply another spiritual con meant to entice gullible egos into believing that performing some kind of parlor trick leads one to true cognitive advancement. Oh, and it makes the guru plenty of money to watch people make utter fools of themselves trying to defy gravity. Never forget the profit factor in any of the realms of mystical or religious spiritual beliefs.

The reader may object to my using the term parlor trick when I refer to levitation, but this is exactly what levitation is, a parlor trick. Go to Youtube again and watch a video called *Levitating Man Trick Revealed* in order to understand how this feat of illusionary magic is performed. Then Google *Levitation trick* to see a wealth of photos illustrating this ancient Hindu practice of sleight of hand. When you can see this practice of ancient Hindu priestly hucksterism, you should ask yourself two questions. Why would any valid religion have to debase itself to perform such illusionary tricks if it had anything of real spiritual value to offer its followers, and why do people still believe such a feat of defying gravity is remotely real and associated with cognitive advancement whatsoever? Whether one is a Hindu priest perpetrating such a fraud or someone who believes this bullshit is possible, you will find no spiritual pragmatism in levitation whatsoever. It is nothing more than a fanciful belief peddled to spiritually-hungry egos seeking a supernatural solution in their quest for spiritual understanding.

This sleight of hand type of priestly magic can be found in Roman Catholic statues that purportedly cry tears of blood or manifest evidence of the stigmata on statues of Jesus, all manipulated of course, by some priest running a pump of chicken or pig blood through hidden channels in the statue. It can further be illustrated by huckster televangelists knocking people over with 'the power of God' in their contrived broadcasts or church services.

The only thing miraculous about any of these feats of parlor magic is that the human ego, with its undying quest for the supernatural, buys this bullshit without question. The alleged story of Jesus turning water into wine can be simply accomplished with a split cask, with one half filled with wine and the other half filled with water. By simply turning a valve from one to the other, any priestly magician could perform this 'miracle'. Now, let us pray. Bleurrghh.

Having challenged such malarkey passing itself off as true spiritual advancement, let's return to that study by Milgram where the test subjects in his psychological experiment would obey orders from an authority and defy them if they came from one they considered a peer, or equal. Within the realm of modern spirituality you will find this same ego-oriented need for authority prevalent in the arena of spiritual pursuits. When trying to explain the principles that I relate in *The Evolution of Consciousness* series in a chat room on a spiritual social network, I found that when someone asked me if I was 'enlightened' and I truthfully responded that I was, there was immediate friction and defensiveness. Egos all over the world are each seeking their own brand of spiritual enlightenment, and they are willing to believe anyone who passes themselves off as an authority on enlightenment, but their egos can't stand the idea that one of their peers can achieve what they have not yet discovered. The ego is inherently jealous and self-superior in its outlook and it can't tolerate the idea that any equal can do what they have not yet achieved where spirit is concerned.

So, let's take a look at some of these so-called spiritual masters and how they present themselves to those to whom they seek to sell their spiritual wares. For a start, let's look at the Hindus, since their religious traditions are older than those in the West. India, like any other country on earth, has a cultural identity which is very closely wrapped up in its religious traditions. If someone wants to present themselves as a spiritual master, they have to present the appearance of an Eastern authority, so they naturally dress in vibrant Indian attire, wearing garlands and other tokens of their religion, or they present themselves with the trappings of the ascetics. Every one of these presentations is a statement made by an ego personality asserting itself through appearance in order to sell a spiritual product. In order for their egos to present themselves as a spiritual guru, they must wear the accoutrements of office to satisfy those who believe in superficial appearances of authority, i.e. they have to look the part.

These alleged spiritual authorities will spew out all sorts of spiritual nonsense telling one how they have to transcend the ego, but their own mannerisms definitively prove that they have not yet transcended their own egos or else they wouldn't have to impress others through such superficial tactics of image projection through outward appearances. Given this truth, then what can any ego know about transcending the ego if it is still in operation controlling one's mind?

Next we move to the Buddhists. Buddhists are very big on talking about defeating the ego, yet the purportedly egoless followers of this religion all present themselves with their own authoritative badges of office, wearing their saffron robes and all with their heads shaved. These purportedly egoless monks are such independent consciousnesses that they all have to wear the same clothes and the same shaved head as their religious cohorts in order to assert their authoritative state of transcending ego. They have each gained such spiritual cognitive independence that the best face they can show the world is the identity of the group ego, but wearing the robes and the shaved head gives them the same air of spiritual authority as the garb of the Hindu Yogis, especially to the gullible Western spiritual seeker. Here again, we are dealing with superficial appearances designed to sow the concept of authority in the minds of the egos seeking authority to provide their spiritual answers.

Within the Catholic faith as well as Islam, the clerics also have their garb of authority, which is simply more superficial presentation that hapless egos latch onto as the clothing of authority. No matter where you look on the planet, there is some sign or manner of garb that denotes the authority figure in virtually every world religion. Protestant Christians may not have the same specific garb as the Episcopalians, Catholics, Church of England and Islam, but wherever you find them you will find the huge cross as their symbol and many people of all these Christian faiths wear their own 'badges of office' by wearing jewelry crosses to tell everyone what they believe or wearing rubber bracelets proclaiming WWJD (what would Jesus do?). Jews do the same thing with the Star of David and Pagans do it by wearing their Pentacle. Every one of these superficial exhibits of faith are nothing more than the ego asserting itself by wearing the symbols of their beliefs to make a statement to other egos what their beliefs are. Not a single one of these items will move them one inch closer to cognitive advancement or any type of true understanding of their own spirit consciousness.

Aside from the superficial manners of dress that present the air of authority in so-called gurus, there are the mannerisms that accompany all the gurus and would-be gurus that populate the New Age spiritual arena. I went to great lengths to describe the mannerisms of the channelers in the New Age in *Demystifying the Mystical,* and I touched on what I am about to challenge now in more depth.

Modern spirituality is rife with the concept that everyone should be perpetually happy and calm. In other words, to be truly spiritual, it seems you need to be, and stay heavily dosed with Valium. These New Age gurus are all professing peace and docility and allegedly avoiding any form of negativity. They all present themselves like any Hindu or Buddhist guru with their smarmy pretentiousness and falsely peaceful demeanors, and egos by the score buy into this superficial nonsense thinking that it is a true reflection of spirituality. The New Age yuppies gather together in their groups, doing their Hindu Namaste bows to each other and putting on the false front of perpetual happiness, but regardless of the superficial fronts they put on for appearance' sake, they are just like every other ego on the planet, playing games with their own minds, deceiving themselves into believing that by comporting themselves in this manner that they are somehow closer to the divine.

The people I have personally worked with and who have succeeded in their own quest for spiritual cognitive advancement can't help but notice how superficial and contrived such activities are. It utterly amazes me how any rational human being can give an ounce of credence to spiritual advancement if such superficial and pretentious people are the spokespersons for spirituality. This is one of the main reasons that materialists refuse to entertain any ideas about spirit presented in these arenas. There is absolutely no spiritual pragmatism in such practices. These examples are nothing more than ego posturing, both on the part of the alleged spiritual masters as well as on the part of the followers of such superficial nonsense. There is never going to be an overall advancement in human consciousness if these people are the model humanity is supposed to follow where matters of spirit are concerned. It is due to such pretentiousness that so many people shy away from spiritual pursuits altogether because, to be utterly truthful, these people look utterly foolish to a rational thinker.

Spiritual advancement is cognitive advancement, pure and simple. There is nothing mystical about the process, only pragmatic processes that can lead anyone to a higher state of cognitive awareness. This process is not about peace or perpetual happiness. It is not about divine love, whatever the hell that is supposed to mean. It is about confronting negativity through a form of deprogramming the indoctrinated ego programs in your own mind. You are not going to go through this process without a certain amount of psychological pain as you confront the illusionary beliefs embraced by your own ego. Through this process of deconstructing the ego hacker program in your own mind, you are going to face varying levels of cognitive dissonance. There is no way around this if you intend to succeed in freeing your consciousness from the chains of your cognitive prison guard. This process comes with a certain amount of psychological pain, and all the love, happiness, avoidance of negativity and docility in the world will not lead you to the enlightenment you think you are seeking.

Having revealed the truth about this process, the egos of everyone wrapped up in these many belief systems will challenge these truths. The ego within you, if you are one of these people, will tell you not to listen to me, to throw this book away and continue to believe what you believe. If you listen to that voice of protest in your own mind, you will never find the enlightenment or spiritual understanding you seek, for advanced cognitive awareness only comes when you can destroy the perceptual illusions you embrace. I don't care if you are part of the ditzy, starry-eyed, smarmy New Age Love and Light crowd, the religious proponents of the supernatural powers of God, or part of the materialist scientific realm who simply denies it all, only pragmatism will lead you to advanced cognitive awareness, not denial.

This chapter would not be complete if we didn't address the modern so-called shamans. Since Carlos Castaneda introduced the teachings of Don Juan to the world back in the late 1960s, shamanism has become another buzz word in the New Age arena. Anthropologists have studied shamans for decades. Tribal shamanism is generally related to the idea that the shaman is able to enter altered states of consciousness to speak with spirits and bring their help into this world. Don Juan used the term Nagualism to describe his teachings, and his teachings have nothing to do with shamanism as it has been studied by cultural anthropologists. What Don Juan taught in matters of spiritual understanding is no different than the guidance we offer in *The Evolution of Consciousness* series. The only difference lies in how the information is being related.

Where Don Juan's teachings were more allegorical and harder to understand, I cut through the mystical-sounding allegory and use modern vernacular to explain the same principles as he taught, as Buddha taught, as Immanuel taught, and as Friedrich Nietzsche tried to teach through his philosophical writings.

Modern so-called shamans are just another variant of the ego personality setting itself up as a presumed authority. Many of these alleged shamans make their claim to fame saying they studied under people like Don Miguel Ruiz, who wrote *The Four Agreements*. Don Miguel is himself just another money making guru peddling more ego feel-good dogma who has set up his own foundation, offers workshops and teaching certificates to those who study under him. In this regard, Don Miguel is no different than any other New Age guru riding on a set of partial but mostly misdirected spiritual principles, making money by bilking the spiritually hungry egos out of their hard earned pay. Those who study in his seminars are peddling the same sort of shamanistic Toltec path mystical nonsense as the Hindus, Buddhists and all the rest are peddling their own brands of spiritual nonsense.

If anyone thinks that they can become a cognitively advanced human being by studying any of this mystical spiritual nonsense, they are only letting their egos delude them. The ego loves to feel good, and any pie-in-the-sky mystical doctrine that will make it feel good provides a wonderful belief that an ego can embrace. Any doctrine that makes an ego feel *special* will sell to multitudes of others. What few people realize in all of this is the similarity in all these false spiritual doctrines. The ego thinks that since the core message is the same in all these teachings that they must be valid. The spiritually hungry ego is so enchanted with the mystical or magical spiritual pursuit that it becomes blinded to the real truth about why all these purportedly different traditions teach basically the same thing, with a few minor variations. The hardcore truth is that it is all contrived! It is an ongoing play of spiritual misdirection designed to insure that people adopt the doctrine of love, happiness and docility, ever-seeking and never finding any spiritual truth of major value. The fact that there is nary a soul in the spiritual marketplace that can, or is willing to tell you these truths, should be a major red flag to anyone seeking true spiritual advancement. If they told you, like I do, that you are individually responsible for advancing your own consciousness without having to buy into their brand of esoteric wisdom or mystical rituals, their mystical con game would end and they would have to get a real job.

What is being peddled as spirituality is philosophical nonsense. Spiritually-hungry egos seek out master after master seeking their enlightenment, yet not a single one of these masters has achieved it any more than the vast majority of people on the quest to understand even what enlightenment is. They are simply salesmen hawking a mystical product and gratifying their own egos by presenting themselves as spiritual experts every step of the way. The ego enchantment with the mystical and divine precludes anyone from ever finding the hard truth, because all of this alleged spirituality is packaged and marketed in such superficial nonsense.

    I ask the reader to ask themselves why none of their presumed spiritual masters have told you even a part of what is being revealed in this book? If they were really any kind of alleged *master*, then where are they exhibiting the spiritual impeccability to show you where the rubber hits the road where cognitive advancement is concerned? Why do they keep running seminars that make them tons of money and write books to support their nonsense, or try to convert you to their own mystical-religious point of view, but not a one of them will tell you how hard it is to achieve what you are seeking? Could it be because they are all only actors on the spiritual stage, selling every listener and reader an ages old bill of goods because their own egos happen to believe the swill they are peddling? I ask the reader to seriously ponder these questions, for it is only through thinking about these questions in a critical manner that you may eventually be led to the truth about spirit. In the harshest light of day, it is all a giant cognitive con game.

3. A World Without Accountability

We live in a world of corruption. It seems to be a running bad joke that everyone knows about but most feel powerless to change. It is because of this knowledge in a growing number of people worldwide that we need to make the move toward cognitive advancement in order to resolve all these problems. In order to stop this corruption, my wife and I have written and will continue to write books, because in order to bring about these changes we need people from all walks of life involved in the process to advance human cognition. We are going to have to reach academics, lawyers, politicians, psychologists, police men and women, scientists, plumbers, architects, judges and any layman that can find the internal courage to make these changes within themselves if we ever hope to stop this running bad joke of corruption that infects the planet.

In order to face and resolve these problems we are going to have to deal with negativity. Anyone who thinks they can avoid the truth of corrupted ego-controlled global societies by embracing love and perpetual happiness as the solution is only deluding themselves. It is nothing but pure escapism.

A major blow to the system was lodged when Edward Snowden dropped the bomb about the NSA spying on American citizens. Many Americans still operating under their national ego consciousness feel that Snowden was a traitor by revealing this information. I guess they don't have a problem with their own government spying on them and gathering personal information just because they can. Aside from the NSA, other information has come forth about the corporations like Google and Yahoo willingly supporting such efforts at spying on American citizen's private phone calls and electronic correspondences, which proves a major collusion between these agencies in all this spying. In truth, these revelations are only the tip of a massive iceberg of corruption controlled by egos whose only goal is greed and control of the world.

As much as many Americans are indulging in their national identity by thinking that Snowden was a traitor, Snowden did the world a great service by revealing what he did. He showed great impeccability by not only discovering this massive spying apparatus, but he endangered his life by exposing it, exhibiting great spirit in doing so. The reporters who ultimately provided this information to the public also exhibited great integrity by releasing it. These people are the kind of people we are going to have to turn into if we ever hope to turn this first cognition tyranny around. It won't be accomplished by smarmy spiritualism and playing the ostrich by hiding our heads in the sand.

We need to find judges and lawyers who can't be bought in order to bring a less chaotic resolution of these problems to ground. We are going to need investigative reporters with spiritual impeccability to expose not only the frauds being perpetrated against humanity as a whole, but who can find the courage to buck the present system of cognition to do so. We need to not only name the perpetrators of financial fraud like Jamie Dimon and other criminal banksters, but insure that people like this are not above prosecution for their criminal acts. We have to remove the political influence of ego-driven people like George Soros from the political arena in every country just because he is rich beyond imagining and can buy politicians, lawyers and judges at will.

We are going to have to work to stop corporate monopolies like Monsanto, which is trying the best it can to corner the market on artificial seed stock through their GMO products. We are going to have to take on ego-driven political activists whose own political ego self-interests drive their agendas. Taking one form of tyranny in the first cognition and replacing it with another will not resolve these problems. Humanity has tried this time and time again and it always devolves into the tyranny of political or religious dictatorships.

We are going to have to pierce the corporate veils and stop simply levying fines on the corporations responsible for poisoning our water and air and food supplies, and go after the decision makers, no matter their position in the corporation, and prosecute them for their crimes with long prison sentences. Corporations are like beliefs, they don't exist except on paper. Corporations are run by people, and people make corporate decisions, and as such, these people are ultimately responsible for their actions. The same holds true for religious institutions like the Catholic Church when it protects pedophiles. Just because it is covered under the umbrella of religion does not give the Pope or any man or woman a free pass to molest children or protect those who do. This is called accountability.

The Catholic Church is the most powerful and richest institution on the face of the planet. It is the silent power behind every central bank on the planet. It is also the greatest real estate holder on the planet. It owns all the land in the Western hemisphere, including the United States and Canada. The reader may think about calling bullshit on this claim, but your disbelief can be short circuited if you simply read the Papal Bull of 1493. In that Bull, written by Pope Alexander VI, one of the Borgia Popes, Alexander VI claimed all the land in the Western hemisphere from the Arctic to the Antarctic the year after Columbus sailed to the Americas. So long as the Vatican is presumed to be any type of power on this planet, this Papal Bull is a legal and still standing precedent of the greatest land theft in the history of the world. It has never been rescinded by any Pope.

There was only a brief period in American history in which this Papal Bull was null and void, and that was after the

Declaration of Independence was signed and acknowledged by France. Once the Declaration was acknowledged by a foreign nation, every contract by any foreign power was nullified and America became a truly free nation, free of the land claims of the Vatican as a result of that Papal Bull, and free of all the King's Charters and land grants issued by the King of England. It wasn't long after the Constitution and Bill of Rights was ratified that an opportunity arose to re-erect the Papal Bull through legal processes. The legal precedent that allowed this Vatican contract to be reinstated was achieved through *Dartmouth College v. Woodward* case of 1819. The foundation for that case, which was heard before the U.S. Supreme Court, arose from the circumstance in which the State of New Hampshire tried to make Dartmouth College a public education facility and tried to appoint its own chosen members to the Board of Trustees of Dartmouth College.

Daniel Webster argued the case on behalf of Dartmouth College and made the assertion that Dartmouth College had been established by a King's Charter in 1769. Webster argued that the King's Charter was a pre-existing contract and that New Hampshire had violated the 'contract clause' of the U.S. Constitution which states that "no State shall impair the obligation of contract." The Supreme Court ruled that the King's Charter was a contract under the law and that New Hampshire could not trespass on that contract based on the 'contract clause' of the U.S. Constitution. Since the King's Charter pre-dated the creation of New Hampshire as a State, the Supreme Court found that the Charter held legal precedence. This was after the Declaration of Independence had effectively nullified all such pre-existing claims by any foreign power.

You may be wondering how the Papal Bull of 1493 has anything to do with the Dartmouth College case. Within the legal system we have a term called inference under the law. The definition of inference under the law states:

> *"In the law of evidence, a truth or proposition drawn from another that is supposed or admitted to be true. A process of reasoning by which a fact or proposition sought to be established is deduced as a logical consequence from other facts, or a state of facts, already proved or admitted. A logical and reasonable conclusion of a fact not presented by direct evidence but which, by process of logic and reason, a trier of fact may conclude exists from the established facts."*

What this law of inference firmly proves is that any contract, previously nullified by the Declaration of Independence to all claims by foreign powers, was thrown down the trash through this interpretation of the 'contract clause' in the Dartmouth College case. By legal inference, every pre-existing contract or King's Charter, including the Papal Bull of 1493 was reinstated by legal inference from the Dartmouth College case. To date, there is not a legal scholar in this nation that I have read that has revealed the truth of this legal chicanery through legal inference. "Part of money collected through the IRS in America finds its way to Vatican coffers in order for the U.S. government to pay rent on all the land in the United States of America that the Vatican secretly owns through the Papal Bull of 1493." Similar taxation provisions can probably be found in most other nations on Earth, and all roads lead to Rome where a percentage of global taxation money is concerned.

Just in case those in other countries are reading this book, let's take the example of England. King John got into a political row with Pope Innocent III over appointing the Archbishop of Canterbury. Without going into all the specific details of the back and forth political rivalry, Innocent issued an Interdict against England in 1208 suspending all Christian services, the administration of sacraments, and the dead were denied Christian burial rights. In other terminology, you could call this a form of blackmail by the Vatican in order to get its way. King John disobeyed the Interdict, after which Pope Innocent III excommunicated King John. The only way King John was allowed to get back into the good graces of the Vatican was to give England to the Pope, after which Innocent III gave him England back as a fiefdom. England became a vassal state to the Roman Church through a political strong-arming property grab by Innocent III, just like the theft of the entire Western hemisphere was prompted by the political greed of the Vatican and its Popes through the Papal Bull of 1493. The Vatican owns Great Britain like it owns all of the Americas and just about every other piece of real estate wherever their missionaries set foot.

The American Revolution may have been fought to break away from King George, but George was just another vassal king working for the Vatican. Americans may have superficially been cut loose from England, but with the exception of a few decades between the acknowledgement of the Declaration of Independence and the Dartmouth College case, America has never been free of this secret Vatican land ownership. This is why people see two Roman Fasces on the walls of Congress behind the Speaker of the House's rostrum. They are symbols of Roman authority and jurisdiction, despite the slogan about 'united we stand, divided we fall' being associated with the symbols. What I have just revealed is the real history behind the *perception* of history we have all been sold. Until the people of the world can tear apart the Vatican and deconstruct its legal and financial stranglehold on virtually every government on the planet, everyone is an unwitting financial slave to the Vatican's perfidy.

I challenge any legal scholar worth his salt to refute what I have revealed here or give me any reason that shows what I presented is not legally sound and binding. So long as any Pope sits on the throne of the Vatican state, these Papal contracts are still legally binding. When you understand this, then you understand why virtually every world leader has to visit the Vatican to pay homage to the real estate mogul that controls the land of all their nations. In political protocol, the sovereign never visits the servant, the vassals always go to sovereign to pay homage. This is why when the Pope visits any nation, he speaks to the people and rarely, if ever, visits the heads of state, because he is the ultimate sovereign over every head of state in the world. Everything else is simply a perceptual dog and pony show to prevent people from knowing these truths.

The present Pope, despite the popularity over his public rhetoric, is the first Jesuit Pope to ever sit on St. Peter's throne in the Vatican. The Jesuit Order, or Society of Jesus as it is officially known, has a very sordid past. In the mid-18th century, the Jesuits were ordered out of every territory under the control of Spain. They were also expelled from Portugal (1759), France (1764) and Austria (1770). In 1773, Pope Clement XIV issued Dominicus ac Redemptor, thereby suppressing the Order.

The Jesuits have been continually involved with political intrigues and financial manipulation since their inception after Ignatius Loyola got the Order approved by Pope Paul III in 1540. The Jesuit Order is the primary driving force behind Liberation Theology in Latin America, the same place that Pope Francis originates. Liberation Theology has been described as nothing more than a form of Christian Marxism, and all Pope Francis's rhetoric about elevating the poor is only the Catholic

Liberation Theology spin on the People's Revolt found everywhere Marxism has reared its ugly head.

Many people are falling away from Christianity at this point in our history, and Catholicism is no less impacted than any other Christian faith. Pope Francis is altering previous Papal protocol in his latest visit to the United States by meeting with heads of State and speaking to the U.S. Congress. Francis is using every public relations ploy at his disposal to redirect people back into his Church and make it valid in the face of a history of pedophile priests and a long history of corruption, murder and intrigue. As with any public relations campaign, this propaganda is only selling to those who demand faith in their religion and those others who want to believe this man is some kind of grand humanitarian. This image is nothing but a perceptual illusion being sold to the masses in order to push forward the Liberation Theology brand of Christian Marxism, hiding behind the mask of holy humanitarianism. It is nothing more than smoke and mirrors founded on manipulating a public perceptual illusion through rhetoric with a serious, hidden political agenda behind it.

There is an unstated political catch to all this humanitarian rhetoric playing on people's compassion. As this book progresses, the reader will see how what the Pope is presently doing is part of a larger and much darker agenda, despite the happy face he is presently using to spin his feel-good rhetoric to the public. His messages are simply pandering to the emotional sympathies of his audience. What he is not telling the public is that all this happy doctrine he is sowing as a Christian Marxist has a political price tag attached to it, and that is not being remotely discussed.

The perception of the Pope's power explains why no one can get into the Vatican or prosecute any of their bankers or priests for the continual fraud they continue to perpetrate. It also explains why the Vatican houses the largest library of ancient historical information in the world and prevents access to this information except to the select few they allow into its precincts. Their Jewish henchmen control the central banks of virtually every nation on Earth. Before you attack me for making this claim, I ask the reader to look at some historical facts. Of the three major Western religions, only the Jews are allowed to charge usury, i.e. interest rates. Christians and Muslims are religiously precluded from the practice and it is not by accident that this came about. It was part of the formulated plan when Judaism and Christianity were being developed side by side during the first centuries around Year 0. I discussed these formative years at length in my book *We Are Not Alone, Part 1*.

Since Christians were precluded from charging interest, every king in the past had to have what was known as a 'House Jew' in order to gain any kind of usury on their taxes. It was deemed a sin by the Popes for a Christian ruler to charge usury and usually resulted in excommunication if they did so. For those who doubt this statement, in 850 the Synod of Paris excommunicated all usurers, as just one historical example. Since the Jews were not Catholics, these excommunications did not affect them. With such power, the Vatican insured that its Jewish banking partners would always remain in control of global finances over all of its territories. It was the Knights Templar, cousins to the Knights of Malta, who were primarily responsible for establishing the system of the modern checking account, and there is valid theoretical evidence that it was the Templars who set up the country of Switzerland as the financial safe haven for their Jewish partners in finance.

By revealing these facts I am not trying to come off as somehow anti-Semitic. I am only sharing historical facts. These facts can be easily verified and they reside in the public domain. Every Jew is not a banker, so don't think for a minute I am trying to level some kind of blanket indictment on an entire race of people based on the actions of a few. But the fact is that the global banking system is all wrapped up in a neat little package, and it all tracks back to the Vatican. We can never hope to resolve such financial tyranny if we are not aware of it.

These bankers and religious hucksters are at the root of most of the financial corruption that we face today. If there is a financial collapse due to the central banks continually printing fiat money, it is the central bankers who should be accountable. If the Pope is unwilling to overturn these centuries old Papal Bulls, then he should also be removed from office and prosecuted for crimes against humanity along with his banker buddies. (Regardless of the Pope's claim to be God's representative on Earth, he is only a man holding the top position of the largest corrupt corporate conglomerate on the planet.)

Every intelligence agency on the planet has deep ties with the Vatican. What we know as the CIA and other intelligence organizations of governments around the planet were started by Vatican priests taking confessions for centuries. Catholic priests used the confessionals to find information to push forward their religious political intrigues for centuries. With the creation of the Jesuit Order we find the foundation for every intelligence agency on the planet. The Jesuits are the spies in plain sight in every nation where they can be found. They have their fingers on the political pulse of every nation on Earth through the confessional and they do not hesitate to be the messengers to their Pope to insure that these secrets are not only kept from their parishioners, but from the public at large.(Is it any wonder, in the face of all this perfidy, why the Mafia is so closely associated with the Catholic Church? Oh, but I guess that is just an accident of religious faith.)

Until we can advance enough humans into the second cognition, this tyranny is going to continue to rule. It is the deceptive rule of the ego demanding its beliefs and denying the truth that allows this crap to continue. To date, the opposition has managed to kill or silence the few voices of opposition raised against their tyranny, but if enough of humanity can get on board for cleaning up this mess and get past the foolish notions that

Jesus is going to come fix it all, humanity may just stand a chance. They can't kill all of us if enough voices are raised from enough quarters, and that is why we need to get this material into the hands of as many people who will listen and work with themselves to rise above all this and finally put a stop to all this first cognition tyranny. It starts with the accountability of individuals perpetrating the crimes, not through fining paper corporations and the luxury of presidential pardons. It starts with *you.*

4. Presumed Authority

The Vatican holds its position of authority due to the perception and belief that the Pope and the Roman Church represent God's authority on Earth. Naturally, Protestants vehemently disagree with this claim by the Pope, but it is, nonetheless, the only claim to power the Pope and the Vatican possess as its seat of authority as a city state. Without people relying on their belief in God and the Pope acting as his spokesperson on planet Earth, the Vatican would fall in a day. Without this claim of presumed authority, the Vatican is nothing but a hollow scam, the biggest con game on Earth. It is a massive organization of global corporate corruption hiding behind the mask of being a holy institution. The only reason the Roman Church is still in business is because first cognition believers keep it operating by denying what their alleged 'Holy' institution actually is. Each of its followers has bought into a perceptual lie, and they will fight to defend this perceptual illusion rather than admit their belief might remotely be in error and that their trust in the Pope is highly misplaced.

The financial power of the Vatican is a reality. There is no shortage of documented evidence of the history of the Church and its politically murderous policies since it came to power to prove this in any court of law. The only thing that remains hidden is the corporate paper trail that leads back to Vatican control. The only thing that keeps it in power is political manipulation provided by its multitudes of front men working to insure that these corporate financial secrets remain secret and the steadfast belief by Catholics that the Pope is the holiest man on the planet.

Behind many of the global intelligence agencies you will find Catholic Knights of Malta, whose membership has held high positions of authority in the CIA, the military industrial complex, the Pentagon and other intelligence services worldwide. The Knights of Malta are also often found as corporate heads in charge of the global corporations, most of which are secretly owned in partnership with the Vatican. People who think that the Roman Church is simply filled with priests and nuns doing God's work are deceiving themselves. I explained fully the origin of the Roman Church and Christianity in my book *We Are Not Alone, Part 1*.

Although the Vatican may be in charge of global financing and corporate monopolism, it is no different than any other religion on the planet where it comes to cognitive control through using people's beliefs in God as an instrument of cognitive tyranny. Islam is just as poisonous to the human mind as is Hinduism and institutionalized Buddhism. Each and every religion holds its power over human consciousness by continually peddling supernatural beliefs or the God dependency. These religions can only maintain their power based on the presumption of authority their priests and imams present to their followers, and this presumed authority, once again, goes right back to the root of Milgram's study.

On the flipside of the religious coin, we find the counter-reaction found in Atheism and stark material science. From these roots we can trace virtually every political 'ism' that further serves to capture and enslave human consciousness through the presumption of authority of its leaders. Through every religion and every political 'ism' on the planet, human consciousness continues to be enslaved under the system of obedience to authority in one form or another. The only ones who rise to power in all of these arenas are those whose egos choose to become the presumed authorities and therefore lord it over the others who have not attained such authoritative power.

In most cases, violence is what enforces the new cognitive paradigm whenever one system of ego control supersedes another. Every religion on the planet has used violence as a tool for conversion to their own brand of faith, and every political 'ism' is no different, regardless of the perceptual illusions it sells its believers. Forcing people to accept any ideology under threat of death has been a powerful tool of first cognition egos throughout time. As a species, we have to advance beyond this type of tyrannical cognitive control.

The only way these systems of first cognition tyranny can continue to rule our minds is through our own fear and ignorance. When people adopt the mindset that, 'You can't fight city hall', they have already defeated themselves and made themselves subjects to the tyranny. When you let fear rule your mind, you are already cognitively paralyzed and make yourself powerless, whether you are going up against religious authorities, political authorities or peer controls in academia. Just saying 'that's how the system works' is nothing more than cognitive defeatism, and the controllers on this planet are perfectly content to perpetuate this mindset in the public. It makes everyone willing slaves to their tyranny. Just because a tyrannical system works does not mean that the system itself should not be challenged and altered. In fact, because a system is tyrannical in nature, it gives us every reason to challenge it - provided we can provide solutions that don't create a different form of tyrannical control to replace the first one. Unfortunately, for humanity operating under the ego control of the first cognition, this is *always* what happens, with no exceptions.

In order to advance into the second cognition, one has to learn that they are their own authority. They have to become a sovereign individual consciousness. This means that you have to stop being a cognitive slave to belief systems erected around you by others. As a sovereign consciousness you are totally responsible for questioning everything and not bending your knee to some principle of authority based on the presumptions of perception." We have people who are experts at their trades, people like plumbers, electricians, architects and lawyers. To become cognitively sovereign does not mean that we disparage professional expertise when we need to call on it, for no one can be a qualified expert at everything. Utilizing the skills of an expert, however, does not mean that our consciousness needs to bow its head to their authority, as is currently the system in place.

I apologize to those in countries outside the U.S.A., for this presentation is most likely going to have sort of an American-centric point of view. This is not because I do not understand that every country doesn't have similar issues, it only means that as an American I can only relate things from my personal experience. So if the reader feels that this is more focused on American issues, it is not. I am using American examples because they are the ones I am most familiar with. Every person living in a different country is going to find similar points of correlation with this data within their own cultures.

Having qualified with the foregoing statements, I am going to use Americans as an example of cultural illusions. This is going to piss of a lot of Americans, but so be it. Outside the U.S.A. there is an impression of America being an imperialist nation based on many things the U.S. government has done that leaves the world with that impression. Most Americans deny these claims because they are operating under a cultural illusion of what America is *supposed* to stand for, which is freedom. Most Americans do not realize that they are probably the most cognitively enslaved nation on the planet, because the happiest slave is the one who most fervently believes he has freedom. The cultural perception embraced by Americans is that as a nation and a people, we represent freedom. The average man or woman on the street believes this perceptual illusion wholeheartedly, but they refuse to acknowledge the tyranny that resides in every aspect of our society through the implementation of our authoritative systems of control.

For many, this illusion of freedom is cloaked in the blanket of religious freedom, which many Americans of faith at this time feel is under direct assault by the forces of Satan who are operating in our government. Few of these people of faith are willing to admit that part of the reason Christianity itself is under assault is due to how Christians present themselves to the public at large, and how the followers of the religion have comported themselves since its inception. They refuse to acknowledge that part of the reason that they are receiving the resistance to their religious beliefs has to do with the actions of the Christians themselves and are not remotely due to the work of the mythological devil. It was after centuries of fighting between Christian sects that the Age of Reason came about with virtually the absolute rejection of religion in favor of science, which has become a religion to the non-religious thinker.

Every religion holds an elitist mentality among their followers. Every follower of every religion believes that the way of their individual religion is the one true way to heaven and the happy hereafter, virtually without exception. It is this ever-present elitist mindset that has caused Christians to feel ostracized in America today. Few Christians are willing to admit that their own actions are causing a lot of these anti-Christian reactions. You can only tell people so many times that they are going to Hell because they don't believe the same way that you do, or that God's going to get you on Judgment Day so many times before you alienate people. Christians have been alienating everyone that isn't a Christian since the religion was created.

It is this type of religious arrogance that has led Christians to be under the spotlight at this time, but few if any of them are willing to admit their own responsibility in creating this friction. Nothing happens in a vacuum, and for every action there is a reaction. Christians have to take responsibility for their actions and quit blaming what happens to them on the devil, just as do Islamics, Hindus and Buddhists worldwide. The New Agers, with their anti-Christian vitriolics, are just another elitist spiritual group of egos working to assert their own brand of spirituality in the same manner, no matter the pretentious front they put on for social group acceptance.

For the most part, Americans generally believe in the merit system, whereby if one works hard and plays by the rules, that they should be able to achieve better goals for their families.

Unfortunately, this system of merit no longer functions due to the greed of corporations and those whose only desire is to control the populace. This aspect of America can be found in every nation on Earth, where corrupt government officials are lining their own pockets and those of their corporate cronies with the tax monies levied from the average working person. The greater their greed, the more taxes are levied in order to support their non-elected bureaucracies, who only add another layer to the hierarchal government tyranny already in place. Most Americans want our nation to mind its own business and not be mucking around in world affairs and wars as our government does. The U.S. government does not listen to the will of the people any more than governments in other nations listen to their citizens. It is a juggernaut controlled by the same money interests that control the IMF, the World Bank and every other central bank around the world.

The American people, contrary to beliefs about America in certain foreign nations, are no different than the French people, the British people, or the average person in every nation on Earth. Every nation is subject to election frauds, provided they even hold elections, and their governments are hard at work to undermine their nations in favor of global money interests who will not be satisfied until they can create a form of global feudalism and force it on the majority of people on the planet so the elite few can serve as our global overlords. The influx of illegal migrant populations in the U.S. from the Latin American countries is no less a threat to the American way of life than the tidal wave of Islamic peoples in Europe. The American government does nothing to stop this illegal invasion of its borders any more than the European governments are working to stem the tide of 3rd world Islamic refugees into their nations.

Because the media in the west is controlled by these elitists, the American people are not told in all honesty that the Latin invasion of illegal aliens is a Catholic invasion, just as the influx of illegal aliens in Europe is an Islamic invasion. Both of these regions of dispossessed people serve the political purposes of the elite to destroy the middle class workers worldwide and alter the complexion and demographics of global societies. If these invasionary tactics succeed, then humanity is very liable to be cast into another era of Dark Ages at the hands of religious zealots and the elitist manipulators who have created these problems.

The elite controllers thrive on generating conflict of any nature, whether it is religious conflict, political conflict, racial conflict, or national and cultural conflict. It is through the implementation of all these forms of conflict that they keep people divided, and so long as humanity stays divided, these globalist assholes will continue to rule the roost where human cognition is concerned. The 1% will continue to control the 99% of the world's population, but all of the blame does not lie strictly with the 1%. The other 99% can only be ruled and controlled through these means of divisiveness so long as they allow this cognitive tyranny to continue. They allow it to continue by embracing their individual beliefs in favor of the beliefs of others, and by allowing their consciousness to be controlled through ego-emotional reactions and manipulations. (There will never be any kind of coming together as a species on this planet so long as people demand to be fragmented and divided.) There will never be any peace so long as these forms of division rule our consciousness.

Those who are in control fully understand how easy it is to manipulate people through toying with their emotions. Mass Psychology, also called Crowd Psychology or Mob Psychology perfectly exemplifies the problem. As Wikipedia describes under the topic of crowd psychology:

> *"This field relates to the behaviors and through processes of both the individual crowd members and the crowd as an entity. Crowd behavior is heavily influenced by the loss of responsibility of the individual and the impression of universality of behavior, both of which increases with the size of the crowd"*

Within this short citation we find the basis for programming the ego personality. It is the utter relinquishment of personal responsibility in the crowd environment that leads to mob mentality. So long as the ego can justify its actions by being part of the crowd and adopting the mass-ego mob mentality, it will always relinquish responsibility for its own actions. One does not have to be present in a crowd, such as with rioters, for this mob mentality of the ego to come into play. Televised propaganda and political sloganism do the same thing to masses of populations in order to sway their opinions based on emotional manipulation. One only has to incite the fear mechanism prevalent in every ego to spark mass reactions. It is exactly this type of cognitive control that sets the stage for every election in every nation on the planet. Every politician panders to the specific desires and fears of their targeted constituency in order to get themselves elected, and it is through control of mass consciousness by playing on ego emotions that every politician comes to power.

The Wikipedia definition of Crowd Psychology goes on to say:

> *"Legal reformers motivated by Darwin's evolutionary theory, particularly in the Kingdom of Italy, argued that the social and legal systems of Europe had been founded on antiquated notions of natural reason, or Christian morality, and ignored the irrevocable biology laws of human nature. Their goal was to bring social laws into harmony with biological laws."*

Here is where every psychologist and social reformer has gone wrong in attempting to understand crowd psychology. The foregoing passage makes the blanket assumption, erroneous as it is, that this behavior is considered to be *"the irrevocable biology laws of human nature."* Accepting this is the gravest mistake that any psychologist ever made. I related in my earlier works in *The Evolution of Consciousness* series that what psychologists presume to be human nature is in fact ego nature. The ego can be defeated and overcome, so any idea that the psychology of the ego is some form of "irrevocable biology of human nature" is the biggest bucket of bullshit any psychologist can believe. If the ego can be transcended and overcome, then it is not remotely "irrevocable biology".

With the ego in charge, there is no such thing as natural reason, and Christian morality amounts to nothing more than indoctrination of principles that give egos embracing Christianity a sense of superiority through their presumed moral behavior. This same sense of religious morality can be found in every religion on the planet without exception. When enough people can transcend the ego and move into a higher state of consciousness, the phenomenon of crowd psychology will disappear along with the insecure and irresponsible ego. When one is no longer governed and controlled through emotional manipulation at the hands of their own egos, and subsequently crowd egos, then this will all stop. When one transcends into the second cognition, they are no longer controlled by these types of ego emotional reactions, and they can't be swayed by the masses through such emotional group manipulation.

The ego validates many of its actions predicated on the premise that since so many others believes as it does, the actions of those in agreement, as well as the individual ego, are justified. The more people who believe something serves as the foundation for the ego in all of us to justify its own actions within the mob mentality. We don't have to gather in masses in the streets in order for the manipulators of human consciousness to generate the ego mob mentality in the individual. They only have to hit the hot button issues that will spark such emotional reactions to sway elections or lead nations to war. If one's personal religious beliefs happen to be the target, the more resistant the ego becomes to anything that challenges that belief. This is the juggernaut we face when working to alter this cognitive paradigm. The indoctrination is so deeply rooted in the ego consciousness that it will fight and even die to defend its perceptual domain. This is why a public dialogue is so profoundly necessary where human cognitive advancement is concerned. Without such a dialogue, then the current crises that face humanity will once again devolve into a massive amount of needless bloodshed, all so individual and group egos can protect their personal or mass perceptions. Nowhere in this present cognitive equation do we find an ounce of spiritual pragmatism, and that is why our presumed authorities need to weigh in on this subject. So long as the ego demands an authority for providing answers to these many crises, it is incumbent on these authorities themselves to engage in such a much needed dialogue. The authority figures, like everyone else, are going to have to transcend their own egos in order to discover that we have been doing it all wrong as a species for a very, very long time.

5. The Band-Aid Solutions

We live in a world where we are surrounded with a multitude of problems. As I have stated repeatedly throughout my works to date, the ego is the ultimate root cause of all of our societal ills, no matter which nation or culture one lives in. Because our experts in psychology have been too short-sighted in getting to the root cause of human psychology, they have all missed any type of solutions to the problems. Our *experts* in the arena of human psychology are too busy making a diagnosis and categorizing what is considered mental illness predicated on the foundation of societal normality which, unfortunately, is predicated on the ego program itself. Our *experts* are too deeply immersed in the ego program themselves to ever see the program for what it is. As such, they can only offer Band-Aid solutions to the psychological circumstances they encounter in the human species.

The first thing I will point out is that there are people with legitimate mental issues, but the ego program is hopelessly ill-prepared for how to deal with many of them. Putting people in mental institutions is a costly endeavor that can impoverish a household in a very short period of time if one of their loved ones happens to have serious mental issues. Some of these mental issues can be treated, but some of them can't. The personality of the psychopath is a prime example, and it is one I'm going to use to illustrate where I am going with this chapter.

People can't understand the psychopathic personality because in general, they have no emotional connection with other people and have no sense or caring about how their activities can negatively impact not only their families, but the public at large. They generally exhibit no real emotions, being totally superficial in their actions. There is an utter disconnect where conscience is concerned with the psychopathic personality.

A psychopathic personality is only interested in their own wants and desires. As such, the public often falls prey to their activities. Many psychopaths are perpetual petty criminals, getting in and out of jail as well as mental institutions through the present revolving door policies of both the legal and mental health systems because one can appear to be totally sane, cogent and educated and, under current guidelines of psychiatry, they are not considered insane according to the definitions of insanity that govern the industry. Many of them have been in and out of the system so much that they know the system better than the psychiatrists who try to treat them.

In the psychopathic personality, there is a disconnect with the world at large, and the public simply becomes a means to satisfy their own individual ends. Psychopaths can be highly intelligent and can lie with the best liars on the planet, so long as it serves their individual needs and desires. They are expert manipulators and con artists. It doesn't matter what anyone else thinks or does, psychopaths are only interested in their own self-gratification, and if that self-gratification amounts to perpetual bouts with the law or the mental institutions, they have no point of connection with anyone but themselves to even care. They are like an ego on steroids, but without the emotional connections, or conscience, that most people have. The can put on a good show, but behind the superficial façade of caring, there is nothing there.

The legal system in America, especially in the last 50 years or so, has turned the mental health industry into a nightmare for anyone who has a mentally ill relative. It is virtually impossible to get anyone committed these days. Mental patients can literally check themselves in and out of the mental wards with the stroke of a pen. The system of laws in the U.S. has turned into a financial grist mill, and it is the legal system itself that has created this mental health crisis in this nation. Unfortunately, and this is probably a worldwide phenomenon where lawyers are concerned, the courts are no longer about seeking justice. Trials amount to who has the best legal 'mouthpiece' in order to sway ill-informed juries to vote in favor of their client. It is all about who can pay the best liar to represent them. Justice is never the issue, it is the win for the attorney that matters most. Lawyers are more concerned with their reputations and making money than their having any sense of seeking real justice. As such, justice has become a meaningless concept in courtrooms worldwide.

In case studies provided by the psychiatrist Hervey Cleckley, in his book *The Mask of Sanity*, Cleckley continually points out the legal insufficiencies that allow the psychopathic personality to basically roam free as a predator in our societies due to the revolving door policy of mental health laws as they currently exist. The subjects in his numerous case studies in the book had a history of being in and out of mental institutions and, in many cases, in and out of jail on a frequent basis. The psychopath learns how to beat the legal system as well as the mental health system and, as such, neither the police nor the mental health care providers have any means by which to deal with these people. Even if they commit a murder, it seems they can fall back on the 'insanity defense' in order to escape justice by preying on a jury's sense of compassion and escaping punishment in prison for their crimes. Psychopaths are consummate actors.

One reason problems such as this continue to plague societies is found in the misdirected ego need to feel compassion. When dealing with psychopaths and recidivist criminals, it is patently obvious that the systems currently in place are woefully insufficient to solve the problems these circumstances demand. In America, the prison system has been turned over to private corporations and prisons are now in the business of making a profit. Many of these private prison concerns have judges who are stockholders in these prison corporations, and they have a vested interest in putting more people in prison in order to see their shareholder profits elevate as more prisoners are incarcerated in facilities in which they hold part ownership as stockholders.

In a case that was prosecuted a little over a decade ago, a judge was brought to trial after an investigative reporter discovered that this judge was sentencing young girls to a detention facility. Once these girls were locked away, they were forcefully prostituted to high level corporate and governmental officials. This is a very sad testimony to the abuse of the legal system in this country, and it also why people fear being dragged into the legal grist mill. When we have judges sitting on the bench responsible for such activities, and lawyers who are only interested in freeing criminals so they can continue to prey on the public, we have a system of legal corruption that needs to be utterly and totally revamped.

At the root of all of this we find the corrupt ego personality, and often times, the mentality of the psychopath. Due to the misdirected ego concept of compassion, generally handed down by religious authorities, our cultures have allowed this type of thing to continue, particularly when the public is unaware of such abuses. When one steps into the second cognition, they realize that this false sense of ego compassion is a major part of the problem. You can only turn the other cheek so many times before you run out of cheeks. Spiritual pragmatism means that one has to address these wrongs in some pragmatic manner. It is patently obvious that the system we have in place is not doing the job. It doesn't matter how many laws they pass, it is the system itself that is sick to the core, and this is all founded on ego greed and egos playing on the sympathies of a jury's compassion that allows this revolving door to continue to function. We are eventually going to have to find a workable solution.

With many judges owning stock in the prisons they sentence prisoners to in order to further line their own pockets, we have a legal system that is designed to frequently prosecute people for very minor crimes, and sometimes even convict an innocent person, because the prosecutor was the best liar in the courtroom that day. In America today, the criminal class has become the perpetual victim and the entire platform of legal logic is being thrown out the window. A criminal burglar can now sue a homeowner for protecting his property by shooting and wounding the intruder, and the criminal can actually win their case as the victim.

The law has been so utterly corrupted by ego greed, using the law as a political platform for lawyers to become a judge because some prosecutor can tout his conviction rate, that the legal system is now virtually defunct of any real value where true justice is concerned. The law has been removed from the average person unless they can bankrupt themselves in order to afford a decent attorney. The office of the public defender is, for all intents and purposes, nothing but the training ground for young lawyers working to eventually make their own practice in the future. "Public defenders" are rarely qualified to step into the shark tank of the courtroom with the more skilled legal prevaricators, and this is one reason that public defenders are basically a laughable excuse for lawyers to most people. Chances are, if you get assigned a public defender because you can't afford to pay the more high-class legal liars, you are either going to be fined or go to jail, whether you committed the crime or not. That is one hell of an indictment against the so-called justice system.

Where the ego personality is concerned, it is not the law that it fears, it is the punishment. I will admit that there are billions of people on this planet who follow the guidelines of the law, but with the ego program in place, all it takes is the right circumstance of inflamed ego emotional passions to take that law abiding citizen and turn them into a murderer through crimes of passion. The latent reactive emotional state present with all egos is like a loaded gun, you never know when the ego might pull the trigger. And no, it is not the gun's fault, it is the ultimate responsibility of the person who pulls the trigger in such cases who is at fault.

Because of this false sense of compassion, we have established rehab centers for people to wean themselves off of drugs or alcohol. Many people who go through rehab have enough self-discipline to keep themselves clean, however, many others don't. People addicted to hard narcotics often turn into criminals, whether they turn to robbing a store, or whether they continually steal from friends or family in order to buy their particular fix, these people are a problem in societies. One might try to make the claim that an alcoholic is less dangerous than a user of crack or heroin, but that is only a form of mental equivocating. It doesn't matter which mind altering substance one uses in order to justify their thievery or abuse of others, it still amounts to an out of control ego personality who only cares about what they want in opposition to anyone else. In the face of these circumstances, alleged moral compassion has to come to a stop and real solutions have to be presented.

  The vast majority of people on the spirit path have this mistaken idea that to be spiritually focused, one has to be a pushover. The starry-eyed mystical concepts about spirituality are not going to solve the tough problems that face the world. It is going to take a harder, more pragmatic set of solutions in order to try and resolve these problems. There are those who will read these books and claim that I have no real spiritual awareness because I don't fit the false touchy-feely image of the superficial guru described earlier. That image is an illusion that has misled people for thousands of years, and such ideas are not going to deliver any solutions to these and many other problems humanity faces at this time. Avoiding hard problems is not a solution.

I want to cite a specific example of not only skewed logic, but how the controlling elements working avidly to undermine the Bill of Rights apply this logic, particularly the 2nd Amendment to the U.S. Constitution - the right to keep and bear arms. America is the only nation on Earth that didn't have the mentality of the 'subject' or 'peasant' being shoved down their throats ever since the American Revolution. Granted, our predecessors all came from countries in which kings or queens ruled over their subjects. Ever since we threw off the yoke of the King of England, no American has ever considered himself a subject or peasant to anyone. With this premise also came the responsibility for one's actions, although it has been terribly undermined in the U.S. today.

There are millions of law abiding gun owners in America today. Most Europeans don't understand what they think is an American fascination with guns. The reason Americans so fervently work to protect their gun rights from tyrannical forms of government can be readily illustrated when you look at rock-throwing Palestinians standing up to machine gun wielding Israelis. When a populace is disarmed, they become nothing more that rock-throwers and pitchfork-wielders in the face of a heavily armed government. The 2nd Amendment assures that every American has the means to combat his own tyrannical government if that need should ever arise. When you can understand this principle and the reason behind private gun ownership, then you can fully understand why the global elite are pushing hard to remove that right to bear arms from the American public. When Hitler came to power he implemented strident laws against gun ownership. The same thing happened in Communist Russia. Now they are trying to do the same in America.

These days, when we find any kind of person hurt or killed by a gun-wielding criminal, it is the gun's fault, not the individual who pulled the trigger. We have a saying in America - "When you outlaw guns, only outlaws will have guns." This is a very true and valid observation. The left-wing (socialist communists) knows that they can't succeed in their desires to destroy this nation and take over the world so long as the people have a means of resistance if they are pushed too far and their freedoms are more obviously threatened than they presently are. Every time there is a gun crime perpetrated by a *criminal individual*, the left-wing gets on the bandwagon screaming about how guns should be outlawed. They have gotten so effective in their manipulations of the legal system that they are now trying to hold the person who sold the criminal the gun liable, although the seller had absolutely nothing to do with the crime and the transaction was perfectly legal.

So let's take a look at the dichotomy in logic. Statistically speaking, there as just as many people hurt or killed by drunk drivers every year as there are by guns. The left-wing media doesn't report this statistical fact because it doesn't fulfill the agenda to disarm a nation through sensationalized incidents of criminal gun violence. Where you see the attempted prosecution of gun sellers or gun manufacturers for providing the instrument that some *criminal* used to hurt or kill another individual, you won't hear a whisper about prosecuting the alcohol manufacturer for making the alcohol that was at the root of drunk driving deaths, although they are trying to prosecute bartenders for serving the drinks. You won't hear this protest because it doesn't suit the agenda for the globalists to bring the U.S. population to its knees to forward their globalist agenda. Until one can view this dichotomy of logic, or let's be honest and call it a double standard, one can't fully understand what is at stake.

To be cognitively advanced means that one can see certain solutions that others operating under ego either can't or refuse to see. These solutions are not necessarily pretty or nice, nor are they wrapped in any false sense of compassion or religious morality. We have to view the psychopath, the murderer and the recidivist criminal as a cancer, for in actuality, that is what they are. They are predators on any civil society. When we can recognize this truth, then we have to start to analyze how to deal with these problems. I know there are millions of people opposed to the death penalty so, in that respect, we have to look at a potential alternative solution.

We do not feed a cancer when it is discovered. We either try to drug it to death or excise it. We are going to have to take the same approach with the predators on our societies. We have to reach a point in our cognitive advancement to realize that we can no longer provide the recidivist criminal with three hot meals a day and a place to sleep out of the weather every night for years or for life. We can't continue to pay for a system that just turns the criminal elements back on society, and this is what the present prison system, particularly in the U.S. has become. We house prisoners, feed them, give them TV and library privileges, give them workout rooms so they can train and make themselves even harder criminals than when they went in, then the system lets them loose on the public. Now, you have to ask yourself, is this how you would treat cancer?

These criminals can not be rehabilitated because they keep committing serial crimes. The leftists are unwilling to admit this fact and still demand that we take a more compassionate approach with these predators on our societies. It is exactly through bullshit liberal treatment of these types of criminals that we have the crime rates we do. They call themselves 'progressives' and hide behind the faux mask of compassion, fully aware of the consequences they are unleashing on the public. But that's okay, it fulfills their political agenda.

Under the current system of legal corruption, what I am about to propose is not reasonably executable for the simple reason that too many egos are at play who corrupt the system. Until we can finally come up with a *real* justice system interested in *real* justice and not just legal chicanery, these propositions are not remotely workable. We have to arrive at a different solution for the legal system than is currently in place.

We have to start enforcing the laws fairly and equally or there is no law at all. When judges have a vested interest in filling the prisons that they own stock in, there is no justice. When lawyers are lying to defend their clients who they know are dead to rights guilty, there is no justice. Ultimately, there can be no kind of real justice rendered by any ill-informed jury that is controlled by their emotions and a false sense of moral compassion. The entire system needs to be revamped from top to bottom, but until enough people can transcend the ego indoctrination, none of these solutions are remotely workable.

For those who don't care for capital punishment, the only viable alternative to remove these cancers from society is to isolate them on a remote island with no chance of escape. We choose an island that has game, fruit-bearing trees, vegetables, and a water supply. At most, we provide them with seed stock to grow their food and nothing more. That is the only comfort one gets when they get exiled there. If you don't believe that the recidivist criminal, murderer or serial killer should not simply be excised with a bullet to the back of the head, this is about your only viable 'humanitarian' solution to remove the cancer. In the case of the psychopath and the criminal recidivists, California came up with the right idea, three strikes and you're out. Leaving someone three opportunities to not remain a cancer on society should be all that is necessary to either reform them or get exiled to the same island with the rest of their cancerous breed. Once removed, there is no coming back and mental illness is not an excuse for criminal behavior. There should be no discrimination between males or females in this regard. Anyone who still believes that women are the weaker of the species should check out the serial killer Aileen Wuornos or any female gang member.

Once these people are removed for being the cancer that they are as the continual threat to civilized societies, they are to be left to their own devices to fend for themselves. When they get on the island, it is every man or woman for themselves, just as they treat the societies they prey on. They are allowed to kill, cheat, maim and scam each other to their heart's content, far, far away from the societies on whom they prey. Once delivered, whether they live or die is no longer the concern of society.

Is this a hard solution? Of course it is, but what we are doing at the present alleviates none of these problems. If we can't mature more cognitively and get past all these ego excuses about humanitarianism, compassion and unlimited second chances, then these predators will continue to lie, cheat, steal and kill the rest of us. At some point we have to say enough is enough. This same provision applies to the crooked lawyers and judges who sell their services to criminal organizations. If they abuse the law to the point that they lie for a predator and put a murderer back on the street, they should go to the island with the killers they protected. This may seem like an extreme measure, but if you think about it, it makes perfect sense because, for all intents and purposes, these lawyers and judges are aiding and abetting criminal activity by lying or accepting bribes to get them off in the first place. In that regard, they are just as culpable and answerable to the public as the predators they fight to set free. So long as these attorneys and judges are working to subvert the system of justice, they are obstructing the law and are as much a part of the problem as the criminals they represent.

Everything we find present in our world society is governed by the self-interests and passions of the ego personality. The only solutions the ego can provide for any of these problems is the Band-Aid solutions, which are not real solutions at all, but only stopgap ploys amounting to nothing more than the Dutch boy holding his fingers in the dyke. They may stem the tide for a while, but sooner or later this system is going to collapse, and when it does, it is going to be very ugly. Although what I have provided as an alternative in this chapter is presently unworkable under the current system, it is not an unworkable solution overall. If people don't like the solution, then take it as an invitation to come up with something better and more workable yourself. At present, it is not really being discussed effectively at all because egos keep getting in the way of real solutions.

6. Fabian Gradualism and Hegelian Dialectic

I noted in my book *Operator's Manual for the True Spirit Warrior* how Fabian Socialism is a major controlling factor in present day New Age spirituality. The co-founder of the British Fabian Society later became a disciple of Helena Blavatsky, named Annie Besant. Annie Besant was very proactive in social theories and unionism in Great Britain, often giving speeches for the Fabian Society as well as for the Marxist Social Democratic Federation (SDF). Annie made her claim to fame working with a friend named Charles Bradlaugh where, in 1877, both were prosecuted for publishing a book by a birth control campaigner, Charles Knowlton. The scandal that resulted is what rocketed Annie Besant onto the public stage. Besant also started what was known as the Malthusian League in 1877, which was a British organization that advocated the practice of contraceptives and the importance of family planning. Although the organization only existed from 1877 to 1927, its inheritors can be found in the modern organization Planned Parenthood, which is very proactive where abortion rights are concerned.

Besant's Malthusian League, as well as Planned Parenthood, found its origins in the Malthusian idea of eugenics. Margaret Sanger, the creator of Planned Parenthood studied eugenics and started many other Leagues to allegedly protect women's rights on procreation, but the basis of Malthusian philosophy is predicated on the theory by Reverend Thomas Robert Malthus put forth in 1798 in his writing, *An Essay of the Principles of Population.* Malthus placed emphasis on the threat that unchecked population growth would be exponential and the food supply would only advance arithmetically, meaning that the poor would continue to breed unchecked and we would eventually run out of food to feed them.

The solution to this problem was to limit the birth rate of poor by the introduction of contraceptives, and later included the concept of eugenics, which put forth the idea that the human race can be made better through selective breeding for desired traits, while those with undesirable traits should be sterilized and prevented from breeding their lower-quality traits into the population. With Planned Parenthood, we find both principles neatly wrapped within this organization's practices. Abortion, rather than being a medical necessity has, to Planned Parenthood, become a form of both population control and birth control according to Malthusian principles found in eugenics.

The way that Fabian Socialism works is patterned on the Roman general Quintus Fabius Maximus Verrucosus Cunctator, who ultimately defeated Hannibal, although Fabius was outmatched in numbers to Hannibal's army. Fabius refused to meet Hannibal's forces in direct battle due to Hannibal's superior numbers, and chose instead to beat Hannibal in a war of attrition. Fabius is probably the first general to use guerilla tactics to gradually whittle his enemy down by hitting Hannibal's supply lines and putting into effect a 'scorched earth' policy to prevent Hannibal's army from feeding off the land as they advanced. It is through such gradualist practices that the Fabian Society made their model for world dominance, and which is plainly evident in the world today through the slow erosion of personal rights and the undermining of nations. The Fabian Creed written in 1887 plainly states:

"*The Fabian Society consists of Socialists.*

It therefore aims at the reorganization of Society by the emancipation of Land and Industrial capital from the individual and class ownership, and the vesting of them in the community for general benefit. In this way only can the natural and acquired advantages of the country be equitably shared by the whole people.

"*The Society, further, works for the transfer to the community of the administration of such industrial Capital as can conveniently be lly. For, owing to the monopoly of production in the past, industrial the transformation of surplus capital have mainly enriched the ...ass, the worker being now ...that class for leave to earn a*

...und fine and wonderful at first glance ...bout challenging the monopolistic one-...n aspect of the Fabian agenda lies in the word 'administration'. Administration in the terms of Fabian Socialism means the erecting of unelected bureaucracies. These administrative bureaucracies are given power once they are created, and because their officials are unelected, the public has no recourse to remove them from office as they do with elected officials.

Col. Edward Mandel House was a close advisor to Woodrow Wilson, and he wrote a book in 1912 called *Phillip Dru: Administrator: A Story of Tomorrow, 1920-1935*. In this book, Col. House painted Phillip Dru as a statist as well as a firm believer of income redistribution. Through the course of the story, Phillip Dru takes over the government, but only as an "administrator". As Wikipedia notes about the book under the look-up Phillip Dru:

Dru casts himself not as a dictator, but merely as an "administrator". The chief of the bureaucracies. His first administrative reform using experts and boards is of the judiciary. He appointed a second board of experts for the reform of laws. He had another board of experts for tax reform, a board for the incorporation of the states into the national government, and a board to deal with the "railroad problem". The old government is cast as a "negative government", a view that is widely held by progressives, even today.

Although the Socialists, um, shall we say Progressives in order to be politically correct, decry the private ownership of property and hide behind the specious principles of caring about the poor, downtrodden masses, it is the socialists, in collusion with the international bankers, that turned over the control of printing money in America to the privately owned Federal Reserve Bank. This occurred on the watch of a Democrat socialist President, Woodrow Wilson, just as the greater percentage of bureaucratic boondoggles that haunt America today were instituted by Socialists masquerading as Democrats. The Democrat party has followed the bureaucratic imaginings of Col. House very well over the past century. House promoted the idea of "socialism as dreamed of by Karl Marx." This totally reflects the agenda of the Democrat party in the U.S. today.

President Franklin Delano Roosevelt promoted the New Deal, creating the welfare system, the Social Security tax system and a load of other bureaucratic monsters. Lyndon B. Johnson, another socialist Democrat brought in his bureaucratic boondoggles under the name of The Great Society. Barack Obama, a former Socialist community organizer who became President has effectively taken government control over the entire health care system in America through Democrat sponsored legislation that was first attempted by Hillary Clinton when her Democrat husband Bill Clinton was President. Bill Clinton was a student of Carrol Quigley's writings, and Quigley is, coincidentally, probably the foremost authority on the Fabians.

In all fairness, it should be noted that the Republicans are not exempt from this creation of more government bureaucracies. Richard Nixon, the alleged 'great conservative' brought in the national speed limit (violating individual state laws in every state), instituted wage and price controls (a primary element of Marxist control), created the Environmental Protection Agency and opened the door to negotiations with Communist China. George Bush signed into legislation the now infamous Patriot Act that allowed unwarranted spying on American citizen's phone and electronic communications without a court order or legal warrant, created the bureaucracy affectionately known as Homeland Security and he was also responsible for a $700 billion bail out for the thieving banks who technically bankrupted America and the world through their fraudulent banking practices. Naturally, the only way the U.S. government was able to underwrite this massive bailout was through borrowing it from the privately owned Federal Reserve bank which leverages the payments through higher taxation policies against American citizens. It seems that no matter where people turn in the world, we are met with similar corruption masquerading as making people safe or making their lives *better*, yet at every turn we find more bureaucratic nightmares appearing and our freedoms disappearing.

The working model for Fabian Socialism is "Educate, Agitate, Organize". What they call education is not about education, it is about political and psychological indoctrination, or the process of slow brainwashing, hiding behind the mask of education. The Fabians formulated their tenets on the Hegelian Principle of 'thesis, antithesis, synthesis'. Although this original concept was created by Johann Fichte, not Georg Hegel, it is still commonly called the Hegelian Principle. In its most simplistic form it means to create a problem (thesis), then create an antagonism to the problem that you created (antithesis) which causes a reaction, and which is designed to bring the seemingly two opposites together (synthesis), thereby arriving at the solution the Fabians wanted in the first place. This is commonly known as Hegelian Dialectics. It is this Hegelian principle that is also used for 'false flag' operations like the Nazi's burning the Reichstag and blaming it on the Communists so they could eventually come to power.

Hegelian dialectics can only work in societies where ego emotions can be inflamed into a state of emotional reactivity. As I have noted, evoking emotional reactions in people due to the understanding of mass psychology, it is very easy for the world controllers to use Hegel's principles against societies. All they have to do is pick a hot button social issue to ignite the emotional flames in people to spark riots, wars and revolutions. (Mass psychology makes the mob easy to predict and it also gives the manipulators the knowledge of how to manipulate people into mob reactions in order to achieve the goals they seek.) As I have stated repeatedly in my other works, the ego is tragically predictable and easily manipulated through emotional reactivity. The current round of manipulated mass psychology being used against the world today is the massive influx of illegal aliens swamping the western world. In this case, Hegel's principles can be viewed in the following manner.

Let me set the scenario that started all this. The global financial system is run by a very few people. Every monetary system on the planet operates by printing fiat money, i.e. money printed out of thin air with no real assets to back up the currency. Wars are a good way to prop up this fiat money house of cards. The world was in a depression before WW II started. The private central banking concerns were in trouble even then, but the investment in war goods by governments going to war serves as a form of collateral to back up the lending of more fiat money to governments. WW II pulled the private central bankers out of that potential financial collapse and set them on the cycle that led up to the 2007 financial collapse. The U.S. government had to loan $700 billion to the banks to keep them remotely solvent because the fiat money machine had run its course. The global financiers knew this was coming as early as the year 2000.

The events of 9/11/2001 served as a temporary financial boost to keep these central banks solvent through the destruction of the World Trade Center, which led to the war in Iraq. The 9/11 event served as the catalyst to start this Hegelian ball rolling (thesis). The Iraq war was planned for future potential by destabilizing the region and creating the current influx of Islamic refugees into Europe. The global financial systems are even closer to collapse today than they were then. Their only hope to keep their fiat money mills cranking out worthless paper currency is to involve the world in another war. The seeds have been sown, through the principle of Hegelian dialectics to bring this war about.

Europe is being swamped with Islamic refugees from Africa to the Middle East. In time, this is most likely going to result in bloodshed on a massive scale as the European nations are burdened with more refugee invaders (antithesis). This will especially be true if any of these refugees are in fact Islamic terrorists or political activists who eventually stir up Islamics against the native populations of the European nations, which is already starting to take shape. With these observations, we have the makings of another brutal and bloody world war and, as many times in the past, it will use religion as the basis for justification on both sides. Out of this potential brutal world war, the world will be expected to seek a different kind of government, which the Fabian Socialists are ready, willing and able to present as an alternative (synthesis).

Every Muslim is not a Jihadist any more than every Christian is a Crusader, but the flames of passion and fear are already being elevated by the Fabian-controlled press everywhere, doing everything they can to start another world war by sowing ego paranoia and inflaming fear and hatred on both sides, doing everything except directly calling for war --- yet. In the meantime, the Fabian globalists keep moving their gradualist juggernaut closer to world domination while everyone stays distracted with their emotional fears being manipulated and kept at a fever pitch.

Wars serve as a more extreme measure of Malthusian population control as it is always the working classes and the poor who are sent to fight and die in battle, rarely the sons and daughters of the select elite class. When you understand what is happening, then it is easy to see the politics behind it all, and you will find elitist Fabian Socialist manipulation and beliefs making all these things happen beyond the conscious purview of the public whose perceptions they continually manipulate to their advantage.

In the United States, the head of the Nation of Islam organization, Louis Farrakhan recently called for a race war against White America. This is how smart Farrakhan isn't, and how the new organization Black Lives Matter doesn't really care about the lives of blacks. The collective population of blacks in the U.S., reported by the U.S. Census Bureau and readily available through the U.S. government website, represents about 13% of the population. I don't care how good of a general you are, 13% does not remotely translate into good odds in a war situation.

Farrakhan and his racist brothers who are working tirelessly to create this revolt, people like Reverend Al Sharpton and former Congressman Charles Rangel, among a multitude of other agents provocateur actively stirring up civil unrest and rioting, are never called down by the media for inciting people to riot. They are the darlings of the liberal socialist media because they are all helping fulfill the Fabian agenda to destroy America and the world, so they, and their administrative bureaucrat buddies, can sit at the top of the heap and dictate how much is a reasonable amount of food to eat or how many rooms a person can have in their house, or how many children they can breed, etc. Wikipedia notes the following about Hegel, who was one of the late Enlightenment German philosophers who died in 1831:

"His philosophy of spirit conceptually integrates psychology, the state, history, art, religion, and philosophy."

Hegel stated this agenda very succinctly when he wrote that the State:

> *has the supreme right against the individual, whose supreme duty is to be a member of the State...for the right of the world spirit is above all special privileges.*

This statement is about as unambiguous as it gets, and it is from such ideals, adopted by Karl Marx, that we come up with Dialectic Materialism which is:

> *"The Marxist theory that maintains the material basis of a reality constantly changing in a dialectical process and the priority of matter over mind."*

So, there we have it. The entire globalist agenda is designed to harmonize two seemingly disparate principles, capitalism and communism, in order to create a new synthetic whole which establishes the priority of matter over mind, or in other words, the New World Order. As Col. House stated through the voice of his character Phillip Dru:

"The strong will help the weak, the rich will share with the poor, and it will not be called charity, but it will be known as justice. And the man or woman who fails to do his duty, not as he sees it, but as society at large sees it, will be held up to the contempt of mankind."

What you have to recognize in this passage is that there are still going to be the 'rich' in this world of administrative bureaucracy, only they will be 'sharing' their wealth as a matter of 'justice' with the poor, who will apparently remain poor except for the largesse of the rich bureaucratic overlords who determine such things. Also note that the word 'charity' is altered through a form of newspeak to 'justice'. We hear the same thoughts being echoed by the Fabian left today as providing 'justice' to the poor by taking from the haves and giving the fruits of their labor to the have nots, who are no longer producers but have been placed in the role of dependents on the State. This is the Fabian concept of justice, not charity, and it is still the statist administrative bureaucrats who are making these determinations by writing the laws and 'sponsoring' and 'lobbying' them to our elective bodies to enact their plan for global domination.

What the reader has to realize is that government creates nothing but more government. Governments do not produce any goods or services (except through bureaucratic controls) and the only way any government makes money to spend is through taking it away from those governed through taxation. Under the Fabian guidelines, there is no such thing as too much government. If the bureaucrats do not feel that you are giving your 'fair share' to the poor and providing them with their brand of 'justice', they will devise new hidden methods to tax you (like Social Security) into delivering their brand of justice to the poor. In the end, this amounts to the redistribution of wealth, which is one of the core principles Fabian Socialism. Of course, their 'naturally selected' rich elite are exempted from this type of taxation, and new loopholes for the rich to escape such taxation are being invented as often as taxes to be levied on the other 99% of the population are imagined and put into force. The only people being separated from their wealth are the average citizens, and this totally fits the designs of our presumed bureaucratic, Darwinian 'naturally selected' overlords.

As much as your mind may rebel at the concept of such a widespread global conspiracy, these are the words and tenets of the globalist conspirators themselves, the creeds of the organizations they created, the philosophical principles that guide them, and the slow destruction of any society through initiating wars, revolutions, riots and undermining any people that get in their way. This is Fabian gradualism in action, and for the most part, it completely escapes the notice of those who are being deliberately manipulated in this manner because it is the Fabians themselves who control every aspect of the perceptions of the world through cognitive manipulation of every ego on the planet.

To this day, Adolf Hitler is propagandized as being a Fascist, but if you look at Hitler's National Socialist party and what he did in Germany to bring its economy back to life while the rest of the world was gripped in a global depression, you will find that he was following Hegel's principles. What Hitler did in Germany is little different than what the Communists did in Russia, and the Jewish Communists have tremendously more blood on their hands than Hitler ever did (but you never hear a whisper of the 30 million Russians killed under the direct order of the Jewish Communist Lazar Kaganovich in the controlled media). I am not a fan or advocate of Hitler, but the fact is that he was a socialist following Hegel's plans, not a Fascist.

What Hitler did in Germany was create a Fabian State where everyone owed allegiance to the Fatherland, with Hitler playing the role of Orwell's Big Brother. The same thing happened in Russia after the Bolshevik Revolution and Lenin with the rise of Communism. The Fabians use different forms of political 'isms' to create the perception that these things are somehow different, but in the end, tyrannical State control and bureaucracies are always the outcome. You never hear the truth about these things through the Fabian-controlled media, for to tell the truth would expose their agenda to the world. We are continually spoon-fed perceptual propaganda to misdirect our consciousness and keep us all under their brand of mind control.

Due to the Fabian principles, its adherents have been fighting a gradual war of propaganda and mind control in order to create a world administrative body to which everyone is ultimately expected to be simply a cog in their apparatchik bureaucratic machine *a la* Orwell's *1984* and the tenets of Karl Marx. This silent and progressive war has been ongoing since the 19th century and it encompasses the control of governments, academia, religion and governs all New Age thinking hiding behind the mask of a false spirituality and its doctrine of Love and Light. This is one major reason why what I describe as the 'doctrine of docility' is so prevalent in modern spiritual teachings.

The Jesuit Order of the Catholic Church is also intimately involved in this 'liberalization' of the world by teaching revolution from the pulpit through the doctrine of Liberation Theology, which is nothing more than preaching the Fabian leftist ideology throughout all of Latin America and seeking to sow revolutionary activities. The present Pope is a Latin American Jesuit, so despite the bullshit holy front he puts on for his Catholic followers to maintain the image of the Church, he is part and parcel of this global Fabian agenda.

The Catholic Church is in league with the racist and revolutionary Latin group called La Raza in the United States, whose main goal is to reclaim everything Mexico gave up after the Mexican Army was defeated and the Treaty of Hidalgo was signed in 1848 at the cessation of hostilities after the Mexican-

American war. These Catholic Revolutionaries feel it is their right to illegally alter the terms of that treaty through mass illegal alien incursions into the U.S and political activism, in association with and full support of the Catholic Church, to gain all the land back that Mexico ceded and sold to the U.S. meeting the terms of that treaty.

Just as the Islamic invasion of Europe is likely to eventually erupt in violence, this Latino Catholic invasion is very liable to serve as a catalyst for another Fabian sponsored revolution or war in the United States if things don't change. Once again, all of this suits the agenda for population control designed by the Fabian Malthusian philosophy. These incidents are also part of changing world population demographics in order to reduce every common man to nothing more than a minor cog in the Fabian globalist machine. Despite their rhetoric, the Fabians do not want to elevate humanity, they want to equalize humanity at the lowest common denominator so they can continue to rule the political roost. We are simply cattle being herded and prodded into the Fabian corral through misdirection and emotional manipulation. Being ignorant of their tactics only makes it that much easier for them to control us. Denying that this is taking place at all only leaves us more prone to their manipulations.

All of these factors play directly into the hands of the Fabian globalists and the public is left intentionally uninformed through control and manipulation of the corporate media, which is nothing more than the propaganda tool for the Fabian globalists. The propaganda mechanism the media is using against the public worldwide can be found in George Orwell's novel *1984* where the concept of newspeak was introduced. Wikipedia defines newspeak from Orwell's novel this way:

> *"It is a controlled language created by the totalitarian state Oceania as a tool to limit freedom of thought, and concepts that pose a threat to the regime such as freedom, self-expression, individuality, and peace. Any form of thought alternative to the party's construct is classified as "thoughtcrime".*

Anyone care for a dose of politically correct speech? It is through manipulating terms and altering language and the meaning of words that the media works tirelessly to brainwash the public into accepting the Fabian terminology and beliefs. The globalist tyrants have coined such ludicrous oxymorons as 'illegal immigrants' to mask the truth that illegal aliens are not immigrants but are in fact criminal invaders violating the immigration laws of every nation they invade. They saturate the public mind with made up terminology like this in an attempt to make people feel guilty by saying they are not being 'humanitarian' if any nation seeks to turn this tide of illegal aliens away. Until the vast majority of people can see and understand this subversive manipulation of language in order for the globalists to attain their goals of world domination, they are only pawns in the game. The global elite can only succeed in this agenda so long as the public stays uninformed of their tactics and systems of control. Each of their control mechanisms is firmly rooted in controlling and manipulating the ego emotional consciousness of the first cognition. Here again we find the controllers playing on the ego sense of compassion in order to steer people into their way of thinking through a form of guilt or shame for disagreeing with their agenda.

Altering the language from Marxist to Socialist to Communist to Progressive is just another form of Orwellian newspeak designed to confuse the consciousness of those being indoctrinated through the redefining of words to suit a hidden political agenda. Marxist Progressives are enraptured with Darwinism for two reasons. The first reason is that the Theory of Evolution utterly removed God from the equation, thereby firing a broadside across the bow of all organized religions. The other more subliminal meaning is that it removes individual responsibility for one's actions and debases it to strictly biological imperatives over which no one has any real control, at least to Darwin's way of thinking. In other words, "We are the way we are because nature made us that way through the process of evolutionary natural selection". Naturally, the elite Progressives of the world feel that they are more 'naturally selected' to guide humanity based on this biological imperative.

They firmly believe that evolution has placed them in this role and their egos fully embrace this delusion, which is why they push acceptance of Darwin's Theory so hard.

Since the newspeak term political correctness was introduced to the western world, we are already seeing the Orwellian idea of thoughtcrime starting to infect the ego consciousness, with people always checking what they think before they utter a word. Through the mechanism of controlling language and dialogue, the Fabian globalists are seeking to make everyone a prisoner in their own minds and thereby cut off any semblance of protest to their political agenda. It is not that far a reach from politically correct speech to advance into thought heresy. This is the foundational thinking behind Marxist Dialectics of materialism over mind. In other terms, it is mandating the materialist world of ego over advanced spirit consciousness. The ego can be controlled and manipulated, the free mind of one's spirit self cannot be manipulated in the same manner.

Aldous Huxley, the author of *Brave New World*, was also an advocate of eugenics, and in actuality, *Brave New World* is a propaganda book designed to push that agenda. Huxley was also a proponent for the use of psychedelic drugs and his works influenced the likes of Carlos Castaneda, who also advocated using mind altering drugs to reach some sort of mystical enlightenment. Huxley and Orwell were, coincidentally, both members of the Fabian Society. For those who still believe that we are not being indoctrinated, I ask how many of you were required to read Huxley's *Brave New World* or Orwell's *1984* during your high school years? Isn't it simply amazing that, out of all the literature of the world, works written by Fabian Socialists are required reading in our schools? In light of that, we have to look at who controls the educational material in our schools. We only have to look to the bureaucratic union of the National Education Association to find the Fabian agenda to control the educational system and the continual brainwashing of our youth. Tell me with a straight face you aren't being indoctrinated.

In a letter from Huxley to Orwell written in 1949, Huxley noted that the Fabian world revolution "aims at total subversion of the individual's psychology and physiology." Can it be stated any plainer than that? Psychologists and psychiatrists are the gatekeepers of the materialist ego consciousness and they define and defend its boundaries of reality. Academics and scientists refuse to entertain any idea of advanced cognitive awareness unless they can couple it with mind altering drug use and/or mysticism, simply because the ego can't remotely understand any level of cognitive awareness except its own.

People will never be able to come together to reach rational and pragmatic solutions to these problems so long as the rich elitist globalist revolutionaries and their lackeys are in control of the media and control the ego perceptions of the masses. People will never be able to come together so long as their ego paranoia is constantly inflamed and manipulated, and so long as they can be so easily manipulated through their emotional reactions. We have all heard the term that cooler heads need to prevail. Unfortunately, there are not that many cool-headed egos running around who are truly open for establishing a genuine dialogue without their own personal ego agenda getting in the way, and that is why spiritual pragmatism is so important.

7. The Other Side of the Coin

At this point the reader may have reached the false conclusion that I am simply another right-wing endorser of the capitalist system of the robber barons of industry, but such is not the case. From the perspective of the second cognition, I see fault in *all* the present systems, of political 'isms', for behind each of them lies the ego personality seeking to gratify its own selfish goals. The socialist elements described in the last chapter cannot function without the financial input from their capitalist corporate contributors. People are being sold a perceptual illusion when they believe that there is some kind of dividing line between these two extremes. Where it comes to global cognitive control of this planet, the controllers have a very incestuous relationship within these seemingly disparate extremes. The socialists can't drive their agenda forward without the money contributed by the capitalists. The only difference between the two is simply public rhetoric and manipulated public perception. The masses of humanity are sold on the *perception* that they are different, but they are not.

To listen to the left-wing socialists in America, you would have to believe that the Republicans are the party of warmongers, yet it was the socialist Democrat Woodrow Wilson who got America into WW I after promises that he would not do such a thing. It was the socialist Democrat Franklin Roosevelt who manipulated the circumstances to get the U.S. into WW II. It was the socialist Democrat Lyndon Johnson who got the U.S. involved in the Vietnam conflict, and it was the socialist Democrat Bill Clinton who got America involved in the war in Bosnia. So these claims that only the right-wing political party is the party of warmongers is nothing but another form of newspeak misdirection. It is simply propaganda.

To the liberal socialist left, the right-wing in America has been termed the 'religious right' as just another newspeak term of disparagement. The alleged right-wing in the U.S. is primarily pro-Constitution and is jealous of their freedoms protected in the Bill of Rights, and they are not all rabid Christians as the left-wing media continually portrays them with their propagandist newspeak. This adherence to the principles of the founding document of the nation puts anyone who believes in Constitutional constraints on rampant government bureaucratic growth flies directly in the face of the liberal socialists who think there is no such thing as too much government.

This sentiment against the Roman Church in particular and Christianity in general is one of the key core tenets of the Theosophy of Madame Blavatsky. I myself find it utterly amazing that anyone can give credence to the idea that the Roman Catholic Church is in any way holy or is representative of any kind of divine principles. One only has to read the sordid record of the Popes, who dug up dead Popes and put their corpses on trial more than once; who initiated Crusades, not only against Muslims, but against other Christian sects that disagreed with the Roman Church doctrine and authority; who made money letting people buy their way to heaven through selling indulgences; and who murdered millions in their Inquisitions, and who warred against Protestant breakaway sects for decades. The Roman Church's Spanish and Portuguese vassal kings sailed the world, and under direct orders of the Popes, conquered and enslaved indigenous peoples wherever they set foot and carried diseases with them that destroyed millions of people who were no less civilized than the Roman Church claimed to be with all its murderous and thieving ways. These kings were given direct orders by the Popes to dispossess any people they found of their property and claim all their lands in the name of the Pope. Given this track record, it is little wonder that the esotericists have such a bone to pick with Christianity in general, but with the Roman Church in particular.

The mindset of all Christians, no matter the denomination or faith, is nothing more than the group ego striving to remake the world in its own image. Islam is exactly the same and every other religion on the planet is also the same. The ego itself is dangerous. The group ego turns the individual ego into a monster, whether it is a religious group monster or a political group monster. Every ego pushes for superiority of its own viewpoint and damned be anyone who disagrees. When the ego can elevate itself to the level of a group ego, then it can really flex its muscles and sooner or later bloodshed is going to occur. The Catholic Church may have started the witch burnings, but Puritanical Protestants have plenty of blood on their hands in that sad chapter of human history at the hands of superstitious religious fervor.

What I am trying to point out here is that on every side of this equation with the ego psyche controlling human consciousness, we find nothing but hate, turmoil, destruction, and fear. I have a friend who put a post on Facebook in response to a post by someone else on the subject of First Contact with another race of beings from the stars. This is what he had to say about humanity in reference to that:

> *"We are definitely NOT READY to have "First Contact" experience with entities from other galaxies. With the plethora against human rights, i.e. intolerance, judgmental attitudes, religious bigotry, & overall asinine ignorance, we are in dire straits. All of the praying, meditating, wishing & hoping hasn't changed the fact that the inhabitants of planet Earth have a long way to go in developing higher consciousness. The*

escalation of HATE across the board has this world in its grip."

This is unfortunately a sad but true statement about humanity at this point. At the base level of all of this hate we find the ego, whether individually or as a group. The group ego is exponentially more dangerous because in the group environment the ego gets bolstered as other egos who share the same beliefs egg each other on, which leads to a frenzy of emotional reactions when the ego feels threatened enough, and which always results in a *kill the heretic* mentality. All it takes is a skillful agent provocateur to stir up a mob into violence; charismatic preachers with an agenda, political activists with an agenda, racists of all varieties with an agenda can each stir up the group ego by inflaming its emotions, and the best emotion to stir people to action is most often fear. Make a mob fearful and fill them with the sense of righteous indignation and cities burn. Make nations fearful and world wars start. It is so utterly predictable that it is frightening when one watches and knows the solution, seeing it taking place day in and day out at every level of present human cognition, but everyone's ears are closed because of their own ego's selfishness and blindness. Only the Fabian globalist manipulators are cognizant of how easy it is to manipulate the human ego psyche, which is why psychology is one of their major weapons for controlling the world's consciousness.

Right-wing, left-wing, my god, your god, rich man, poor man, male, female, black, white, yellow, brown, red, old, young, union, non-union, Democrat, Republican, Communist, Capitalist, Zionist, Muslim, Christian, Hindu, Buddhist, gay, straight -- ego, ego, ego! Is there any way to better point this out in a manner that people will listen to and see where all this turmoil lies? Does anyone really *want* to listen? At this juncture, I think not. To listen and change one's self requires work and we live in a world which is more interested in handouts of free money for no work than working for something that could elevate an entire species to new, as yet unimagined higher levels of cognitive functioning as a species. We are not responsible for our own actions. Either God is ultimately in control or evolutionary biological natural selection is in control, but in neither case do we find anything but an excuse to not take responsibility for advancing ourselves and our own consciousness. Either God or Nature is to blame for the way we are, and no matter which direction we choose, the ego is totally content to believe this and not do a damned thing to change itself. It just falls in line like sheep behind the bellwether and continues down the road to self-destruction, with some individual or group ego thinking it has all the answers every step of the way.

This species, operating under the ego program, would rather kill each other for beliefs that are merely illusions rather than find any *real* solutions. If people could learn to govern themselves with higher level cognitive awareness through accepting personal responsibility for their lives without seeking external authorities to hold their hand every step of the way, this world could be a much better place for everyone to live. With the ego in place, nations spend the fortunes of the taxes they collect in order to make more efficient killing machines than choose to elevate the hungry to a higher standard of living. They pay farmers not to grow crops while part of the world goes hungry. The people and the governments of the world sit idly by while government agencies like the CIA and the Knights of Malta are the biggest drug running operations on the planet, and the superficial government in the U.S. lies and says it is involved in a 'war on drugs'. Such hypocrisy is only imaginable when egos are in charge. Drug money is the slush fund so the CIA, the Mossad and other 'intelligence' agencies that can then in turn purchase illegal weapons and arm rebel factions around the world, just as came to light with the Iran-Contra affair. All of it ultimately fuels the Fabian world revolution.

The left-wing socialists arm the Communists and the right-wing parties arm the anti-Communists, and the unscrupulous arms dealers, Israel being one of the primary illegal weapons brokers working in collusion with the Russian mob and the CIA, don't care who they sell the weapons to or where they are going, so long as they get their money. You have tinhorn dictators all around the world who, as soon as they get in power, start stuffing their own pockets living in the lap of luxury, whether they are Communists or Capitalists, leaving their people scraping for a living in the street. Here again, welcome to the Fabian New World Order, controlled by people who are eyeball deep in all these escapades against humanity, and who think they are uniquely suited to rule the world based on Darwin's evolutionary biological imperatives.

These would-be rulers know there is no Godly retribution coming in the manner that religionists believe. They know that there will be no judgment day of the manner that Christians believe. They own the courts, the lawyers, the politicians, academia, the drug companies (both legal and illegal), the corporations, the media, and they own your very consciousness in one form or another. They control everything including your individual ego perceptions, and you let them do it by refusing to entertain any idea that goes beyond your own ego's fear and selfishness. It doesn't matter if they sell the illusion from a church pulpit, a mosque, a synagogue, a political podium, in the halls of academia or from a presidential palace. Every concept you embrace as a belief is under their control, but only so long as you allow it to continue. You have the power within you to stop it. You have the power within you to overturn the tyrant in your own head that allows these controllers to control your very consciousness. If you would truly see a better world, a world of genuine peace and prosperity for all, without all the evils of the selfish ego continually dragging down our entire species, then you have to make a choice to make yourself better than you are, better than the hateful, fearful and insecure ego that controls your own mind and subsequently controls the entire planet.

8. The Robber Barons

In the late 19th century, people like John D. Rockefeller, Jay Gould, James Pierpont Morgan, Andrew Carnegie and others earned the title 'Robber Barons of Industry' because they all got so rich that they created monopolies in many industries. Through their avaricious monopolistic practices, they basically held private wars with each other to see who could become the richest man in America and who could glean the most benefit from the others to further their own financial holdings. This episode in American history, through these men's brutal monopolistic tactics and exploitation, laid fertile ground for British Fabian Socialism to counter their actions with their own.

The Fabian Society got replanted from Great Britain to America in 1895. Fabian Socialism finds its roots in the British East India Company (BEIC) which was founded in 1600 and dissolved in 1873. BEIC made many of its stockholders (many of them Freemasons) a tremendous amount of money and they became financiers. John Stuart Mill was the secretary of BEIC from 1856-1873. Mill and many of the other financiers from the BEIC promoted Fabian philosophies. Mill was close friends with

Richard Potter, who was the father of Beatrice Webb, one of the core Fabian Society members.

Although the Fabians were students of Karl Marx, they realized that the Marxist principle of Revolution by the proletariat was unworkable as proven by the working classes of the world not being able to unite during WW I. The Fabian Society's agenda altered from Marx's revolution ideology to one of subterfuge through infiltrating societies and governments from within and through using the principle of gradual non-violent evolution into Marxist ideologies rather than direct violent revolution, a principle known as Cultural Marxism.

The Fabian Society was comprised of many Capitalist backers along with other well to do intellectuals of the time. George Bernard Shaw, one of the early members of the Fabian Society wrote that the methods the Society utilized were "*stealth, intrigue, subversion, and the deception of never calling socialism by its right name*". Their ultimate goal is subversion of all world societies into their own brand of socialism through gradualist indoctrination (brainwashing, newspeak) and, when the time is right, they intend to strike when the moment is most opportune to finally put their idea for a global government in place.

Although John D. Rockefeller was one of the original industrialist Robber Barons in America, his son John Jr. was of a different cut of cloth. During his college years, John Jr. took nearly a dozen courses in the social sciences, including studying

Karl Marx's *Das Capital* (source Wikipedia - John Rockefeller Jr.). John Jr. helped set up many trust organizations for philanthropic work, but many of these organizations were designed to fulfill the propaganda agenda of reshaping society to Fabian ideologies. This Fabian Socialist agenda has continued over the decades through the Rockefeller Foundation. John Jr. provided funding for many Fabian socialist-oriented programs and created the Council on Foreign Relations, which is primarily a Fabian Society think tank and whose members can be found serving in positions of the U.S. government (like some kind of revolving door policy), the press and as captains of banking and industry. Rockefeller Jr. was also a major advocate of Woodrow Wilson's League of Nations idea, and the Rockefeller family donated the land on which the United Nations buildings reside today.

David Rockefeller, the son of John Rockefeller, Jr., studied left-wing economics at the Fabian Society's London School of Economics. Rockefeller is a known member of the infamous Bilderberg group, which has been a Fabian organization from its inception. David's brother, Nelson Rockefeller, served as Republican party vice-President under Gerald Ford. The Bilderberg group was created by a Polish Socialist by the name of Joseph Retinger who is known to be a close associate with the Fabian Society. As you should see, the Fabians make no party distinctions pursuing their global political agenda.

The Rothschild's, who many conspiracy theorists think are behind some kind of specific Jewish conspiracy, have definitive ties with the Fabian Socialists and the left-wing press in Great Britain. Lord James Arthur Balfour was a member of the British Labour Party, which was created by the Fabian Society. It is Lord Balfour who composed the infamous letter to Baron Walter Rothschild that became known as the Balfour Declaration, which served as the foundational document to create the Zionist state of Israel. For all intents and purposes, Zionist Israel is nothing more than a Jewish Marxist-Fabian state created out of thin air through political manipulation, despite what Christians believe about it being some kind of prophetic inevitability of God's people returning to the Holy Land.

The fact of the matter is that Zionist influence in the U.S. government brought pressure to bear against President Harry S. Truman, and it only took 11 minutes after Israel declared itself to be a state for the U.S. President to recognize it as a legitimate state before the matter was ever discussed openly with any other world leaders. It was this rush to judgment that has led to the problems the world faces in the Middle East today, all at the hands of Fabian Socialists working in collusion with Zionist interests to eventually establish a global government over which the Fabian elite intend to rule.

In order to win Christian support for the Zionist cause, Christians were told that the prophecy of the Bible about God's people returning to Israel was being fulfilled by the Fabian-controlled press, and through this means of propaganda, Israel won the unswerving support of American Christians. Most Christians in America still pledge their undying support for the Zionist political state, blissfully unaware of this manipulation and with no knowledge that most of the so-called freedom fighters that established Israel were in fact Eastern European Jewish Communists. Apparently, Christians never realized that the Fabians were quite familiar with this biblical prophecy, and Christians never cottoned to the fact that they had their perceptions manipulated in order to fulfill a hidden Fabian agenda. Christians never dreamed that an unlimited control of money and control of the press was utilized to brainwash them into accepting this manipulation as anything more than a fulfillment of biblical prophecy. Of course, this is exactly what the Fabians and the Zionists had counted on from the start in order to play on the gullible sensitivities of uninformed Christians. In other words, the Fabians intentionally created this appearance of prophecy being fulfilled and sold the idea to American Christians, knowing full well that such manipulation would be readily accepted by people of faith who are ever seeking prophetic biblical validation for their beliefs and who would never question what really happened.

The Fabian Society was formulated by wealthy and middle class people, and those who were part of the middle class soon elevated their own financial status as a result of this collaboration. The Fabians have used the universities worldwide as nothing but indoctrination mills to achieve their global subversive agenda. Through financial and political control of both political parties in the U.S., their juggernaut of political gradualism slogs ever forward without the majority of the population ever figuring out what's happening.

In the Socialist countries in Europe, they sow the seeds of dissent against American Capitalists, all the while European Capitalists are using socialism to hide behind. In the United States, the seeds of dissent are sown against Socialism, while it is the Socialist Capitalists who are manipulating mass perceptions through ownership of the news reporting agencies across the spectrum. People worldwide are being manipulated by all the agencies and corporations the Fabian sympathizers own in collusion with the Vatican, and that includes the socialist agenda of the present Pope. These people can only continue to rule the majority of humanity so long as the average person either ignores what is happening around them, or so long as they continue to believe that it is only one segment of the world's population that is behind this hidden tyranny.

The Fabian operative themselves are the agents of disinformation that keep conspiracy theorists claiming that it is the Freemasons or the Jews, the Communists or the Capitalists, the Illuminati and the Bilderbergs, etc. They are in the business of seeding disinformation from all quarters in an attempt to keep people from ever figuring out how massive and interwoven their agenda actually is. There may be some minor doctrinal disputes within the Fabian ranks from time to time, but regardless of these disagreements, the endgame is what matters most to all the participants and their plan moves inexorably forward beyond the perception of most of humanity.

The American Civil Liberties Union (ACLU) was created by Fabian Society members Norman Thomas and John Dewey. (John Dewey is primarily responsible for the manipulation of the educational system in America that has led to the dumbing-down of our children and our society as a whole through Fabian propagandizing and rewriting history to suit their ends.) The Fabians can only keep themselves in power so long as they maintain themselves as the most educated class on the planet, and therefore justify their actions and fulfill their ego-driven agenda to rule the world over the ignorant masses. The Fabians have no interest whatsoever in elevating humanity, despite all their smarmy rhetoric about the 'greater good'. They are completely in the business of setting up a global socialist feudal state wherein they firmly believe they are ultimately suited to control the destiny of all mankind.

Many Rockefeller and other Fabian-oriented trusts contribute to National Public Radio, which has become one of the main mouthpieces for the Fabian socialist agenda. Its television associate is the Public Broadcasting System (PBS), which started out as National Education Television which was owned by the Ford Foundation, which is also closely associated with the Fabian Society and its global political agenda. One of the primary tenets of the Fabian Socialists is that of education, but what they call education is nothing more than indoctrination through incessant gradual and subtle propaganda to brainwash people into accepting their own political ideologies.

The Fabians, despite their socialist agenda, include many so-called conservative politicians within their ranks. Because they are the intellectuals, they have to continually produce more intellectuals who can fulfill the agenda of their global plan. The Ivy League colleges like Yale University have become the breeding ground for the Fabian production of more intellectual fellow travelers to meet that agenda. Their political ideology is that of controlling both political parties through financial contributions. This concept of buying elections originated with John D. Rockefeller. The Fabians adopted this principle and it is the money of Fabian Society fellow travelers that manipulates elections by making it a war for dollars rather than a process of political integrity. No one comes to power through the American elective process any more unless they are the chosen political darlings of the Fabian socialists. The appearance of any kind of opposition between the right-wing and the left-wing in politics is simply a perceptual illusion sold to the masses to make them believe there is actually any kind of real difference and that they have any kind of choice at the polls when they vote. This is not just happening in America, it is the same worldwide wherever there is an elective process in operation. In totalitarian states it is a non-issue. At the end of the day, they all pay homage to the same master and the Fabian agenda moves inexorably forward.

When right-wing Republicans are in power they are called the war mongers by the left-wing liberal socialists, yet every war that may be started and put into motion fulfills the Fabian agenda of world population control. War is just an added bonus in their philosophy on eugenics, and the Fabian military contractors make billions by arming all sides in these wars. The Fabians are not remotely interested in how many of the 'unwashed masses' wind up dead as a result of the wars they create, because it suits their agenda for population control without them ever having to come forward to admit what their real agenda actually is. The common man is nothing more than cannon fodder to their own plan to achieve total global governmental supremacy by creating their socialist State. There is no war on this planet that is not instigated by Fabian agents provocateur in order to foment those wars.

The Fabians, as noted, work through the process of subversion and alteration of people's perceptions. They use a process of slow, propagandized indoctrination to their ideas, always masking them in the philosophical logic that their way is the kinder, more humanitarian way things should be done. They use this perceptual velvet glove to hide the murderous iron fist of their true actions and hidden agenda. Regardless of all their smarmy philosophical rhetoric about humanitarianism, compassion, and manipulation of the public consciousness through sowing dissent amongst the masses, their agenda is one of total and absolute global tyranny. These elite-minded intellectual monsters are not interested in elevating humanity, they are only interested in controlling humanity through brainwashing the world to their way of thinking, which has always been a form of Marxist Statism.

The worldwide disenchantment with governments, particularly in the West, are all designed to dovetail into the Fabian global takeover. Their philosophy is that in order to destroy national sovereignty, the nation is better destroyed from within by 'the will of the people', rather that from external sources which might meet with resistance. What the general population doesn't realize is that it is specifically through Fabian manipulations that these governments have become the tyrannical juggernauts that those governed are protesting against. This all goes back to the Hegelian Dialectic of thesis, antithesis, synthesis whereby the Fabians are creating these government monsters by corrupting the elective processes in the first place. They then use their controlled media outlets to broadcast the corruptions present in the governmental structures that they manipulated into being in the first place, by 'exposing' this corruption to the masses, thereby controlling the public perception and herding the population down the road of the Fabians' choosing. Through these means of perceptual manipulation of our consciousness, people are led to believe that they are starting some sort of grassroots movement against the government, yet they do not see that these movements are being controlled by the same Fabian manipulators.

Many people worldwide have figured out that there is really no difference between political parties other than the rhetoric they sell the public in order to get elected. With what is revealed in this book, more people should now understand why there is no apparent difference between the parties, because in the final tally, it is the Fabian globalists themselves, all working in collusion with each other, who control every side of every argument. In doing so, the Fabians can play all sides against each other and the populace at large is not remotely aware of how they are being manipulated through emotional divisiveness sown by the Fabians to ultimately achieve their plan to control the world. So long as people believe it is this side against that side, which the Fabian instigators all ultimately control, they remain unaware of the singular agenda of the Fabian organization itself. The public perception is constantly being 'agitated' by these intellectual tyrants who think the world is their pearl and who believe that the greater part of humanity is only their slaves and labor pool to further enrich themselves.

Through the manipulation and control of the mass media, people's consciousness is constantly bombarded with this type of cognitive assault. The public is sold the concept of dualism and, unfortunately, operating under the first cognition, the people are blissfully ignorant of how they are being emotionally manipulated through mass psychology at the hands of these tyrants. Everyone's consciousness is so fraught with emotionally manipulated reactivity, that they can't get past their emotions to see through to what is actually taking place with the Fabian brand of cognitive manipulation. It is because of this emotional reactivity that the Fabians can predict which way the public mood will shift in almost every situation. So long as we, as a species, continue to be emotionally reactive operating under the first cognition, such manipulation will continue to take place and the masses will continue to be herded like cattle into the Fabian global plantation.

9. Fabian Socialism and New Age Indoctrination

Within a great percentage of the New Age assimilated doctrines, we often find the concept of *Service to Others* put forth in much of the material. Many people within spiritual movements worldwide, including Hinduism, Christianity, Buddhism and the New Age have their heads filled with the idea of compassion. The concept of spiritual compassion is coupled with an altruistic desire to save the world, professing that it is only through compassionate understanding of other people that one's own spirituality is therefore enhanced and made more valid. They believe they are serving God or the Divine principle through serving others.

This Service to Others concept is a double-edged sword that most people who believe in the doctrine do not realize has a darker and more sinister form, and that is using spirituality and the Service to Others concept as a springboard into a Fabian Socialist, Orwellian 'Big Brother' form of global government. The Theosophical Society is really big on promoting this Service to Others doctrine and, given what was noted previously about the intimate connection between Fabian Socialism and Theosophy, this concept has to be viewed in a more harsh light than the fluffier spiritual version of Service to Others that pervades New Age thinking.

As I described previously, Fabian Socialism is founded on the principle of the slow indoctrination, or brainwashing of people into their particular worldview. This is achieved through a newspeak type of cognitive manipulation that is designed to redirect people's thinking processes down the avenues that lead to the Fabian form of indoctrination through psychological manipulation. In essence, they are peddling a form of perceptual altruism whereby they convince people that they are working for the 'greater good' when they embrace this Service to Others indoctrination. We need to view this type of indoctrination from a different angle to understand what is really going on behind the faux spiritual teachings they promote to the masses.

The believers in the Fabian Socialist doctrine are all fully convinced that they are ultimately suited to rule the world, and that their perceived form of governance is the best idea on which to model the world to control the rest of global society. Under the idea of a global socialist system of control, eventually everyone will be part of and working for the Fabian State, which will have supreme control over all the land and every individual as stated in their creed and further emphasized through Hegel's principles of the individual being erased in favor of the personality of the State.

Once everyone is drafted into being nothing more than an actor for the State, simply becoming a cog in their materialist cognitive machine, they will already be indoctrinated into the Service to Others concept as the highest attainable goal one can achieve. It will keep everyone's focus centered on maintaining the 'greater good' through continual Service to Others with the Fabian Socialist State as the primary definer of what the 'greater good' means at any given point. You have to realize that this indoctrination is a slow process, and I can use the analogy of putting a frog into a pot and slowly turning up the heat to boil it rather than tossing the frog into boiling water and trying to jump out of the pot. The Fabian principle is exactly the same. Through misdirection and a process of slow cognitive indoctrination through redirecting and manipulating our perceptual awareness, people eventually become brainwashed into accepting the Fabian's principles as a matter of form, never realizing that they are being psychologically manipulated at all.

Hiding behind the Theosophical 'spiritual' teachings, millions of people worldwide are already being indoctrinated with the Fabian Service to Others mentality which, in time, can easily be rolled into people being nothing more than supporting State functionaries using the same principles. That is the hidden dark agenda behind these false spiritual teachings. The believers in the doctrine are already in the pot and the water is heating up, but they are not remotely cognizant of what will happen when the water hits the boiling point. They are all swimming around in the pot accepting the Service to Others doctrine thinking they have some special edge on spiritual understanding without ever realizing that they are being cognitively manipulated into subliminally accepting the Fabian political ideology by embracing this alleged 'spiritual' doctrine.

A compilation of essays was released in 2013 in a book entitled *Pathological Altruism*. Although I don't agree with most of the ideas posited in that series of essays, one of the concepts introduced was about the altruist who thinks they are doing good things for humanity (or others), but whose designs are ultimately harmful to the people they think they are helping. I think the Fabian/Theosophical agenda is a prime example of this type of pathological altruism. Through the medium of New Age spiritual teachings, they are peddling this form of pathological altruism to the masses masquerading their true political agenda as some form of spiritual truth. If they succeed, New Age religion will ultimately replace all other religions as the accepted State religion of the Fabian concept of Orwellian nirvana.

Outside this indoctrination through the alleged spiritual arena, the Fabian lawmakers are already corrupting the law, particularly in the United States, to convert all law into administrative functions through a process called Administrative Procedures. At the present time, most lawyers think that Administrative Procedures only apply to bureaucratic or administrative agencies. What they don't realize is that if the Fabians succeed in their plans, every facet of the law will be nothing more than an extension of the Fabian State's administrative stranglehold on global society. The most defining case in U.S jurisprudence on the subject of administrative law is found in the case of *United States v Mersky, 361 U.S.431, 1960.* The following quotes all come from this U.S. Supreme Court decision and should fully illustrate the creeping devolution of the law through enacting administrative procedures.

> *"An administrative regulation, of course, is not a "statute." While in practical effect regulations may be called "little laws," they are at most but offspring of statutes."*

What this short passage relates is that administrative rules are primarily definitions created to define the boundaries and applicability of a statute. You have to remember that administrative processes are just a different way to describe bureaucratic processes, and for any type of bureaucratic system of government to work, every bureaucratic division has to have its controlling rules.

Under statutory law, unless it is determined to be too broad and undefined in its scope, or is found to be unconstitutional, a statute applies to everyone, not just bureaucratic administrations. Through the creation of the Administrative Procedures Act, the Fabians and their socialist allies are in the process of altering statutory law into administrative bureaucratic law. Under the present perception, administrative rules only theoretically apply to the bureaucratic agencies themselves, but this is an illusion. The advent of administrative rules and regulations is now in the process of undermining statutory law as the primary law that most nations once adhered to in favor of this administrative legal blurring of the lines. This is most evident in the following observation issued by the high court in the Mersky decision:

> *"The result is that neither the statute nor the regulations are complete without the other, and only together do they have any force. In effect, therefore, the construction of one necessarily involves the construction of the other."*

Where, for hundreds of years, statutory laws have been quite sufficient to allow the legal system to function, this passage in the Mersky decision has now debased statutory law to only be effective if an attendant administrative regulation is created to give it the force of law. Do you see the reversal taking place here? Statutory law is no longer good enough, we have to have a bureaucratic administrative rule to now 'define' who the statute applies to and under what conditions. Through such legal maneuvers, the law itself has become subservient to bureaucratic control.

Under the Administrative Procedures Act (APA) in the U.S., virtually all statutory laws have become ineffective and meaningless unless there is a bureaucratic definition, an administrative rule, to give the statute the force of law. Legally speaking, under the APA, the statutes can only truly be enforced against those defined in the regulations, however the courts are presently ignoring this administrative corruption. Let me give you an example. Every state in the United States was basically compelled to enact some form of the Model APA. The most populace states like California, Illinois, New York and Florida, for example, have highly developed administrative procedure rules and regulations. Other states have adopted the model, but have not gone as far as creating this administrative legal nightmare within their own borders as these states just mentioned. These governing administrative rules on the Federal level are found in the Code of Federal Regulations (CFR).

In one of those states with a highly developed APA in which I once lived, I had a friend get ticketed for a traffic violation. We went and researched what the State administrative regulations defined as to whom the statute applied. Within the definition of the State APA, the particular statute my friend was cited for, under the regulations, only applied to school bus drivers. My friend was not a school bus driver, so going by the Mersky decision, the statute would not apply to him. When my friend went to court and challenged the judge according to the State's administrative definitions, the judge played stupid and claimed complete ignorance of the administrative procedures definition and to whom it applied. This was State law and the judge was expected to be apprised of the laws of the State over which he was paid to adjudicate, yet he claimed stone ignorance of the matter.

The importance of this story is to show the reader a couple of things. Administrative Law is just one more aspect of creeping Fabian Socialism undermining our legal systems worldwide in order to create their future bureaucratic control. This subversion is going on beyond the purview of the average citizen and, unfortunately, most lawyers and judges. Since this law is in its transitional phase, it has effectively nullified statutory law and made the law meaningless because their regulatory administrative rules have not yet been fully established nor has their Fabian form of global government yet been enacted to shift all law into their designed administrative mode of State control, but have no doubt, they are working tirelessly, plodding ever forward through their gradualist agenda to achieve this goal.

The problem that most people have in regard to trying to figure out this global agenda is that they all fall prey to a sort of compartmentalization of facts, a type of cognitive tunnel vision. They only see what they want to see and refuse to see how what they personally believe might remotely be a part of what is happening around them that they are protesting against. As I noted in my other books, a lot of highly valid research into these things has been done by Christian researchers and others who do the research because their own belief structure is threatened. What happens with this type of tunnel vision is that the researchers see only what they want to see, but don't see how their own perceptual beliefs can be part of the problem as well. This is a form of cognitive selective denial. Until one can remove the dependency on their own beliefs, thinking that they are somehow sacrosanct and free from this cognitive tampering, they are only looking at the bottom corner of a painting and not seeing the full picture.

Eastern spiritual traditions, which have also been adopted into the New Age doctrine, are big on stating that everything is connected. What they do not see with this belief is that every avenue of cognitive manipulation happening on this planet truly is connected. There is no avenue of human consciousness that is not connected through the manipulation of our perceptions. No belief is pure, no political ideology is inherently correct, and the most unpragmatic idea we can embrace is that our own belief structures are not being manipulated by others to herd us in the direction they want us to go.

In order to expand our cognitive awareness, we all have to broaden our horizons. We can't continue to only criticize the parts of the picture we disagree with and leave our own personal beliefs out of the equation thinking that they have not also been tampered with, and then think we are going to see the full picture. So long as we continue to believe that we are not being manipulated on every front where our conscious awareness is concerned, we will never see the full picture. (Saying that all of the world is screwed up except what you personally believe will leave you forever blind to seeing that part of the cognitive manipulation and deception. This is that selective denial I am talking about.)

For the conspiracy researchers, it's not the Illuminati, or the Vatican, or the left-wing, or the right-wing or the Jews. It is not the Muslims and it is not the Christians. It is not the Hindus and it is not the Buddhists or the New Agers. It is *all of these things.* There is not one part of present first cognition perception that is not being manipulated by someone, and that includes what you personally believe. At present, there are very few people worldwide who have seen that much of the larger picture. They are all focusing on smaller parts of the painting without seeing the whole shebang. That is one of the reasons I am writing this book, to show the reader what spiritual pragmatism is and what reaching expanded awareness really entails. It is a tough and dirty road to come face to face with all of these things, but so long as one refuses to see that their own personal beliefs are a part of it, they will still be cognitively enslaved to some aspect of the first cognition system of manipulation and control over their consciousness.

Selective denial will not free your mind. The ego will still rule your consciousness so long as you demand embracing its own brand of perceptual reality. The ego is the inherent root problem found in all these avenues of cognitive manipulation. The ego governs the consciousness of the pathological altruists of the Fabian ideology, and the ego governs the consciousness of those who unwittingly believe their doctrines thinking they are spiritual truths. The ego controls the minds of every religious adherent on the planet, and the ego controls of the minds of the academics, politicians, scientists and every layman on the street. The following chapter should bring this all into focus.

10. The Prime Example

I have stated repeatedly that we find the ego and its fear, arrogance and selfishness behind every problem we face on the planet as a species. I came across a letter being widely circulated and a newspaper article written in England that proves every point I have been making. Although this letter originates in England, I think it safely sums up the feelings of the majority of the people worldwide who are suffering under the influx of refugees and foreign immigrants, no matter their nationality.

Within the following passages you are going to find not only the ego mentality of the composers of the letter and news article, but they are a reflection of the ego selfishness of foreign elements who demand what their egos demand in return. In the midst of everything presented below as well as the ego-driven mindset of the foreigners who refuse to assimilate and demand adherence to the cultures they left behind, when everything else is removed, there is only ego.

"*I want My England Back.*

Please keep it circulating!!! (To other countries if possible as well as: " ENGLAND "

I think this really sums it all up.

After hearing that many cities did not want to offend other cultures by putting up Christmas lights, so DIDN'T!

After learning that the British Red Cross shops were instructed not to display Christmas decorations lest they cause offence. (A move which cost them and all likewise thinking "my" support thereafter.)

After hearing that the Birmingham council changed its opinion and let a Muslim woman have her picture on her driver's license with her face covered. (You try it and be identified by Police etc!)

After hearing of a Primary School in Birmingham where a boy was told that for PE they could wear Football League shirts (Aston Villa, Birmingham, West Brom etc) but NOT an England shirt as it could offend others !

This prompted the editorial below written by a UK citizen, and published in a British newspaper."

"IMMIGRANTS, NOT BRITONS THAT MUST ADAPT!!!

Take It Or Leave It. I am tired of this nation worrying about whether we are offending some individual or their culture. Since the terrorist attacks on London, we have experienced a surge in patriotism by the majority of Brits.

However, the dust from the attacks has barely settled and the 'politically correct' crowd begin complaining about the possibility that our patriotism is offending others.

I am not against immigration, nor do I hold a grudge against anyone who is seeking a better life by coming to Britain. However, there are a few things that those who have recently come to our country, and apparently some born here, need to understand.

This idea of England being a multicultural centre for community has served only to dilute our sovereignty and our national identity. As Britons, we have our own culture, our own society, our own language and our own lifestyle. This culture has been developed over centuries of wars, struggles, trials and victories fought by the untold masses of men and women who laid down their lives and of the millions of men and women who have sought freedom.

We speak ENGLISH, not Spanish, Lebanese, Arabic, Chinese, Japanese, Russian, or any other language. Therefore, if you wish to become part of our society, learn the language! (This does not apply to English people who chose to work overseas, they have already planned to come back HOME to UK.)

If God offends you, then I suggest you consider another part of the world as your new home, because God is part of our culture, which is most of the population. If St. George's Cross offends you, then you should seriously consider a move to another part of this planet.

We are happy with our culture and have no desire to change, and we really don't care how you did things where you came from. This is OUR COUNTRY, OUR LAND, and OUR LIFESTYLE, and we will allow you every opportunity to enjoy all this.

But once you are done complaining, whining, and griping about Our Flag, Our Pledge, Our National Motto, or Our Way of Life, I encourage you take advantage of one other great British freedom, 'THE RIGHT TO LEAVE'.

We didn't force you to come here. If you don't like it: GO HOME, OR SOME WHERE ELSE!!

You asked to be here.. So accept the country that accepted YOU. Pretty easy really, when you think about it. If we all keep passing this to our friends (and enemies) it will also, sooner or later get back to the complainers, lets all try, please.

No matter how many times you receive it....please forward it to all you know!!!

If you don't want to forward this, you are not only "PART OF THE PROBLEM", you are subjecting your grandchildren to rule under "NON" ENGLISH Rule!!

Make this Christmas as visible as possible!"

Within this passage we find every element of the ego exhibited, just as I have described it in every book I have written. We find the complaints of the individual ego as well as the statements of the ego as a group through the usage of such terms as 'my' and 'our'. If you come here this is 'my' country, this is 'our' religion, this is 'our' culture, this is 'our' flag, this is 'our' rule. Every ego in every nation on the planet has the very same sentiment. The refugees are no different because they demand to keep 'my' religion, 'my' culture, 'my' feelings are to be considered in favor of 'yours' and 'I' demand to be catered to on 'my' terms. I challenge any reader, particularly the experts, to show me how the ego is not behind all of this, and also how it can be effectively disproved that the ego is not the underlying core problem to every issue that faces humanity at this time.

In all fairness, I completely understand the position of the writer of what was presented. In actuality, every culture on the planet pretty much demands the same thing of others who resettle in their nations. Every country expects the newcomer to conform with or tolerate their cultural norms, and to date, this has not been an unreasonable demand. But if we are ever going to turn into a more viable species without all these divergences, these ego attitudes are going to have to change. Instead of continually fighting for 'my country and my god', it should be 'this is our planet and we need to make everyone as prosperous as possible'. I am not remotely talking about the same kind of global consciousness that those who are driving the globalist agenda are seeking to implement, for their agenda ends with tyranny, where what I propose, leads to freedom of consciousness for all, without the paranoid territorial and cultural imperatives demanded by the ego. Is this a utopian dream? Perhaps, but it is not unattainable, once we can remove the ego from the equation.

Every ego on the planet demands that its perceptions be catered to by others. If it is a group ego in the form of nationality, culture or religion, it is only reinforced and becomes more rigidly adamant where its demands are concerned. It is exactly due to this arrogance of the ego to protect its perceptual territorial domain that wars are started and continue to be fought - all because every selfish ego wants what it wants and damned be anyone who refuses to give it what it demands.

In order for humanity to advance, we are eventually going to have to use one common language. English is already the language of Aviation and also the language of Science. English is one of the main secondary languages taught in

European schools and it is the primary language of the US, the UK, Australia, Canada (except for Quebec), South Africa, and is usually the primary second language studied in China. Short of creating another language, humanity is already moving toward using English in areas of commerce as well. As a species, I think it would be advisable to capitalize on this and expand it so that as a planetary society, we can all start to speak one language. So long as we have the vast diversity of languages, we are always going to have problems of mistranslation and, therefore, misunderstanding. This suggestion does not arise from any sense of Anglo-centrism, but from observing the fact that we are already moving in that direction anyway. I see no harm in working to expedite this process in order to help us move forward as a planetary species and, in truth, it is a common sense approach to the problem of language diversity which keeps us divided and continually misunderstood.

I challenge any academic scholar, psychologist or psychiatrist to provide one iota of believable evidence to counter these observations. This is the truth of the world we live in and it is the ego program itself that is at the root of everything that plagues this planet today. No one operating under the multiple layers of indoctrination that shape the fictional ego personality can see through this problem because they are all so deeply held under their own ego's control to see the solution. They are all so immersed on their own ego perceptions to see beyond their own selfish desires, whether they be individual desires or those of the ego acting within the group mentality.

The egos of the alleged *experts*, with all their education, are most likely going to protest the hardest because, with all their laurels and degrees, not a one of them has seen this problem. The psychologists and psychiatrists can cite Freud until the cows come home, yet not a one of them, *not a single one on the entire planet,* has seen what I have described about the ego, because their own egos inflate their sense of self as an expert on the subject. They are too blinded by their own ego arrogance to even remotely solve this problem. Academic and professional hubris will make them protest at every turn because what I have revealed in all of these books puts all their alleged expertise right in the dumpster. With the exception of Friedrich Nietzsche, every philosopher alive and dead has missed this. Carl Jung, a noted metaphysical psychologist got close, but close is not good enough. Other than coining the term Ego, Sigmund Freud didn't have a clue what the ego was, and neither do any of the psychologists and psychiatrists who cite that sexual deviant father of psychiatry as an authority. They are all utterly clueless, and yet they are the gatekeepers of normality and sanity on the planet. The ego in all its facets is the greatest mental disorder on the planet, and everyone is infected with it, *including* the experts on mental disorders.

As with everything I write, I am providing the reader with tools to sow awareness. We can never solve the problem if we don't identify the problem. The problem is the ego and it is readily identifiable within every person on the planet who has not advanced his own consciousness beyond its control. This is the path to enlightenment, the road to higher level cognitive abilities that removes one from the morass of the ego world so they can identify the core issue that every ego on the planet fails to see. Most of the time, one must view a problem from outside in order to identify the problem. Like you, I spent most of my life under the perceptual control of my own ego. I could no more see the solution then, no matter how hard I tried, until I had destroyed its control over my own mind. If I can do it, so can you. It takes diligence and determination and, as Nietzsche described it, a "will to power". This is the path to Willful Evolution as an individual and, ultimately, as a species. *This* is spiritual pragmatism.

Afterword

Right now, I am like a piece of flotsam floating above a dark sea of ego consciousness. My own consciousness has risen above this dark and gloomy sea, as can anyone else who has the courage to change himself. I can see that 'dark cloud of humanity', as Friedrich Nietzsche described it, and it is not a pretty picture. As that quote from my friend said, I see a world full of hate and it is escalating exponentially. It is like a raging boil waiting to burst vile ego pus all around the planet. The books that we have composed in *The Evolution of Consciousness* series along with the companion volumes may be too late to change things. The juggernaut of the ego that demands destruction may be too powerful to change. Each day can bring the start of another massive global conflagration and all I see is people driven by their own egos who think they know everything, yet who truly know nothing about what humanity can be without the ego to rule their consciousness.

The people of the world, all people, need to do some serious soul searching in order to find the spirit that lives within themselves. If humanity shows no desire to find that truth hidden within them and chooses to continue to live their lives embracing perceptual lies, then maybe its best if the species does destroy itself so someone else can start over with a better chance of success. This piece of flotsam, floating on this sea of ego hatred and paranoia, selfishness, greed and corruption, can only look upon this dark sea with dismay and disgust. Even though I have shown examples of the problems that plague us as a species, as well as exposing the absolute rock bottom root cause of all of the crises facing humanity, I have serious doubt that many will listen. I would sincerely love to be proven wrong in this assessment.

This book presents many painful truths to face and to psychologically come to terms with. No matter how much one wants to deny a global conspiracy, especially predicated on media propaganda against conspiracy theories, you have in your hands some of the words of the conspirators themselves as well as examples of how they are seeking to achieve their goals for global control. If you don't want to use the word conspiracy because you find it objectionable, call it a *plan* for global control. In truth, there really is no difference except the perception of the words. There is no shortage of information that goes into substantially greater depth on the matters presented in this book if one is inclined to dig it out. Unfortunately, most egos are too lazy to do anything except stay cocooned in their own selfish desires in their own little ego perceptual world, texting, social networking or living with a cell phone plugged into their ears most of their waking hours..

I have tried to present this information in a civil and cogent manner, rather than use the firebrand type of conspiracy revelations used by so many egos who often have a tone of panic in their presentations and who sometimes advocate violent solutions to every situation in which the group ego feels threatened. This sense of panic plays right into the hands of the Fabian globalists and it is extremely counterproductive to the advancement of human consciousness This tone of panic usually arises because the ego presenting the information feels that their religious or cultural beliefs are threatened by what is happening in the world and can only think as the ego always thinks, and that is to react emotionally and defend its own territory.

We have illustrated throughout *The Evolution of Consciousness* series what the problem is and how to resolve it on a personal level. Until enough people can address the issue of the ego on a personal level, humanity will continue on the same self-destructive course it has throughout time, occasionally offering Band-Aid solutions, but never really curing the root cause of the disease. The work begins with you, the individual. Only when enough individuals can finally see the world with greater clarity and finally admit the truth will the world situation start to change on a greater scale. Until that happens, there will be more needless bloodshed and political chicanery to manipulate people into wars and genocide. It is the ego beast we need to conquer in all of us if we ever hope to see a solution to these problems and finally see humanity evolve into a more civil and genuinely peaceful world. So long as the ego controls our individual and global consciousness, we will never make this world of peace. We will only talk about peace with an eye to war and destruction for every idea that challenges our own limited ego perceptions.

At this time, I am only one small voice in an ocean of ego control. The question is whether this voice will be heard in time, or whether it will be heard at all. Only you can decide that for yourself. As for myself, this bit of flotsam seeks a different shore, a place where our consciousness can finally come to rest in a land of peace and prosperity for all, without the ego manipulating and mandating its own limited interpretations of that reality. This place is not an escapist fantasy. It will have to be built, for at present, this place does not exist. In fact, such a place cannot be remotely imagined within the selfish confines of the first cognition land of the ego. We are all potential builders of this new land, but it won't be built if everyone decides that the present system of cognition is acceptable, unalterable and continues to fight to defend it. It won't be built so long as everyone continues to avoid their personal responsibility by placing it on others to make their decisions for them. For every ego that relinquishes this responsibility, there will always be controllers like the Fabians and their allies that will take that responsibility that you relinquish and shape the world to their own ego desires while the rest protest, riot and die in formulated wars so the controllers can continue to rule you beyond your conscious awareness.

About the Author

The author of this book has great concerns about the direction the world is headed. He has written numerous books on the advancement of consciousness and what humanity can do to remove itself from the cognitive tyranny that keeps everyone's consciousness enslaved.

The Evolution of Consciousness Series

Book 1

A Philosophy for the Average Man: An Uncommon Solution to a World Without Common Sense

Book 2

Willful Evolution: The Path to Advanced Cognitive Awareness and a Personal Shift in Consciousness by Endall Beall

Book 3

Demystifying the Mystical: Exposing Myths of the Mystical and the Supernatural by Providing Solutions to the Spirit Path and Human Evolution by Endall Beall

Book 4

Navigating into the Second Cognition: The Map for Your Journey into Higher Conscious Awareness by Endall Beall

Book 5

The Energy Experience: Energy work for the Second Cognition by Mrs. Endall Beall

Book 6

We Are Not Alone – Part 1: A Challenging Reinterpretation of Human History

Companion Volumes
by Endall Beall & Mrs. Endall Beall

Recovering Spirit After the 2012 Disappointment: Spirit Pragmatism Beyond the Realm of Mystical Fantasies by Endall Beall

Operator's Manual for the True Spirit Warrior by Endall Beall

Spiritual Pragmatism: A Practical Approach to Spirit Work in a World Controlled by Ego by Endall Beall

Future Books

We Are Not Alone – Part 2: Advancing Cognitive Awareness through Historical Revelations by Endall Beall

Clarifying the Don Juan Teachings For the Second Cognition: A Pragmatic Reanalysis Without the Mystical Misdirection by Endall Beall

Advanced Teachings for the Second Cognition by Mrs. Endall Beall

Parenting for the Second Cognition by Mrs. Endall Beall

Revamping Psychology: A Critique of Transpersonal Psychology Viewed from the Second Cognition by Endall Beall & Mrs. Endall Beall

Index

1%, 71
1984, 109, 112
2nd Amendment, 85
9/11, 100
Abortion, 92, 93
Accountability, 52
Administrative Law, 142
Administrative Procedures, 138
Administrative Procedures Act (APA), 141
Administrative rules, 140
Afterlife, 27
Age of Reason, 68
Aliens, 36
American Civil Liberties Union (ACLU), 129
American Revolution, 56
An Essay of the Principles of Population, 93
Archbishop of Canterbury, 55
Atheism, 65
Authority, 29, 30, 31, 34, 39, 63, 65, 66
Balfour Declaration, 126
Balfour, Lord James Arthur, 126
Bankers, 59, 96
Banking system, 60
Beliefs
   Definition, 15
Besant, Annie, 92
Bilderberg group, 125
Bill of Rights, 53, 85
Black Lives Matter, 102
Blavatsky, Helena, 36, 92, 115
Bolshevik Revolution, 106
Bradlaugh, Charles, 92
Brave New World, 111, 112
British East India Company (BEIC), 123
British Labour Party, 126
Buddha, Buddhism, 25, 26, 36, 41, 46, 69

Institutionalized, 65
Bureaucracies, 31
Bush, George, 97
Carnegie, Andrew, 123
Castaneda, Carlos, 45, 111
Catholic invasion, 71
Catholics, Catholicism, Catholic Church, 52, 58, 61, 64, 107
Central banks, 60
Christian morality, 74
Christians, Christianity, 27, 36, 58, 59, 64, 68, 74, 115, 116, 126, 135
CIA, 61, 64, 120
Cleckley, Hervey, 80
Clinton
    Bill, 97, 115
    Hillary, 97
Code of Federal Regulations (CFR), 141
Cognitive advancement, 38, 44, 87
Cognitive defeatism, 66
Cognitive dissonance, 16
Cognitive selective denial, 143
Cognitive tyranny, 72
Columbus, 52
Compassion, 80, 88
Confessions, confessionals, 61
Congress, 56
Consciousness, 23
Constitution, 53
Council on Foreign Relations, 125
Criminals, 88
Crowd psychology, 72, 73, 74
Crowley, Aliester, 36
Crusades, 116
Dark Ages, 71
Dartmouth College, 53, 56
Dartmouth College v. Woodward, 53
Darwinism, 110
Das Capital, 125
Declaration of Independence, 53, 54, 56

Democrat party, 97
Dewey, John, 129
Dimon, Jamie, 51
Don Juan, 45
Dru, Phillip, 95
Ego, 111, 116, 144
   Emotions, 99
   Nature, 30, 74
   Personality, 16, 17, 27, 32, 33, 40, 46, 72, 81, 83, 84, 91, 114, 153
   Program, 24, 34, 153
Election fraud, 70
Elections, buying, 130
Elite controllers, 71
Elitist mindset, 69
English language, 152
Enlightenment, 25, 34
Environmental Protection Agency, 97
Escapism, 49
Eugenics, 93, 111, 131
Excommunication, 59
Fabian
   Creed, 94
   Socialism, 92, 98, 105, 136
   Socialists, 101
   Society, 94, 123, 124
Fabianism, 109
Fabians, 108, 124
False flag, 99
Farrakhan, Louis, 102
Fear, 118
Federal Reserve, 98
Federal Reserve Bank, 96
Festinger, Leon, 16
Fiat money, 60, 99, 100
Fichte, Johann, 98
First cognition
   Egos, 26, 66
   Tyranny, 62, 66

First Contact, 117
Ford Foundation, 129
Freemasonry, 36
Freud, Sigmund, 154
GMO, 51
Gnosticism, 36
God, 63, 110, 119, 135
   Belief in, 64
Google, 50
   Levitation trick, 38
Gould, Jay, 123
Greed, 34
Guns, 85
   Ownership, 86
Hannibal, 93
Hegel, Georg, 98
Hegelian Dialectics, 98, 100, 132
Hegelian Principle, 98
Hell, 69
Hindus, Hinduism, 36, 40, 65, 69
   Priesthood, 26
Hitler, Adolf, 86, 106
Holocaust, 28
Homeland Security, 98
House Jew, 59
House, Col. Edward Mandel, 95, 96, 103
Human nature, 30, 74
Humanitarianism, 58
Huxley, Aldous, 111
I AM movement, 36
Illegal migrant populations, 70
IMF, 70
Immanuel, 27, 46
Impeccability, 48, 50, 51
Interest rates. *See* Usury
IRS, 55
Islam, Islamic, 108
   Refugees, 100
Islam, Islamics, 36, 64, 69

Invasion, 71
Israel, Zionist state of, 126
Israelis, 85
Jesuit Order, 57, 61, 107
Jesus, 27, 39, 62
Jews, 60
Johnson, Lyndon B., 97, 115
Judaism, 59
Judgment Day, 69
Jung, Carl, 154
Juries
   Ill-informed, 79, 89
Justice, 79
Justice system, 83
Kaganovich, Lazar, 106
King John, 55
King's Charter, 53, 54
Knights of Malta, 60, 64, 120
Knights Templar, 60
Knowlton, Charles, 92
La Raza, 107
Law of Attraction, 34
Lawyers, 80, 89
Legal system, 88
Lenin, 106
Levitation, 37
Liberation Theology, 57, 58, 107
Logic, 86
Loyola, Ignatius, 57
Mafia, 61
Malthus, Thomas Robert, 93
Malthusian League, 92
Marx, Karl, 97, 103, 124
Marxism, 57, 58, 124
Mass Psychology, 72
Mental patients, 79
Milgram, Stanley, 28, 32, 39, 65
Military industrial complex, 64
Mill, John Stuart, 123

Mind control, 20
Mob mentality, 72
Modern spirituality, 42
Monsanto, 51
Morgan, James Pierpont, 123
Mossad, 120
Muslims, 59
Mystical monasticism, 26
Mysticism, 37
Nagualism, 45
Namaste, 43
Nation of Islam, 102
National Education Association, 112
National Education Television, 129
Nazi Germany, 28
New Age, 18, 36
   Doctrine, 143
   Religion, 138
   Spirituality, 92
   Thinking, 136
New Agers, 69
New Deal, 97
New World Order, 103
Nietzsche, Friedrich, 46, 154, 156
Nithyananda, 37
Nixon, Richard, 97
NSA, 50
Obama, Barack, 97
Obedience to Authority, 29
Orwell, George, 109
Paganism, 36
Palestinians, 85
Papal Bull of 1493, 52, 54, 56
Pathological Altruism, 138
Patriot Act, 97
Pedophiles, 52
   Priests, 58
Peer review system, 31
Pentagon, 64

Perceptions, alteration of, 131
Personal responsibility, 120
Phillip Dru: Administrator: A Story of Tomorrow, 1920-1935, 95
Planned Parenthood, 92
Pope, 60, 63, 64
   Alexander VI, 52
   Clement XIV, 57
   Francis, 57, 58
   Innocent III, 55
   Jesuit, 57
   Paul III, 57
Population control, 101, 108, 131
Potter, Richard, 124
Pragmatic
   Definition, 22
Pragmatism, 45
Predators, 88
Prison system, 80
Prophecy, 126, 127
Psychedelic drugs, 111
Psychopathic personality, 78
Public Broadcasting System (PBS), 129
Public defender, 83
Quigley, Carrol, 97
Quintus Fabius Maximus Verrucosus Cunctator, 93
Rangel, Charles, 102
Recovering Spirit After the 2012 Disappointment
   Renamed *False Prophecies, Reassessing Buddha and the Call to the Second Cognition*, 26
Religion, 65
  Morality, 74
  Zealots, 71
Retinger, Joseph, 125
Right to bear arms, 86
Rockefeller
  David, 125
  John D., 123, 124, 130
  John D. Jr., 124

Nelson, 125
Rockefeller Foundation, 125
Roman Church, 63, 64
Roosevelt, Franklin Delano, 97, 115
Roswell, 36
Rothschild, Baron Walter, 126
Ruiz, Don Miguel, 46
Satan, 27
   Forces of, 68
Second cognition, 23, 25, 61, 66, 74, 114
Selective denial, 144
Service to Others, 135, 136, 137
Shamans, 45
Sharpton, Al, 102
Shaw, George Barnard, 124
Snowden, Edward, 50
Social Democratic Federation, 92
Social Security, 97, 105
Socialist Capitalists, 128
Socialist Progressives, 96
Society of Jesus, 57
Soros, George, 51
Sovereign consciousness, 66
Spirit
   Definition, xi
Spiritual advancement, 44
Spiritual masters, 48
Spiritual pragmatism, 18, 75, 82
Statutory law, 140
Stigmata, 39
Supernatural, 39
Supernaturalism, 36
Switzerland, 60
Synod of Paris, 59
Taxes, 70
Televangelists, 39
The Four Agreements, 46
The Great Society, 97
The Mask of Sanity, 80

The Secret, 34
Theory of Cognitive Dissonance, 16
Theory of Evolution, 110
Theosophical Society, 135
Theosophy, 36
Thomas, Norman, 129
Thoughtcrime, 111
Three strikes, 89
Toltec path, 46
Treaty of Hidalgo, 107
Truman, Harry S., 126
U.S. Congress, 58
U.S. government, 70
U.S. Supreme Court, 53
United States v Mersky, 361 U.S.431, 1960, 139
Usury, 59
Vatican, 52, 53, 55, 56, 57, 59, 60, 61, 63, 64, 128, 144
Violence, 65
War, 101, 131
Webb, Beatrice, 124
Webster, Daniel, 53
Wicca, 36
Wilson, Woodrow, 95, 96, 115
World Bank, 70
World Trade Center, 100
Wuornos, Aileen, 90
Yahoo, 50
Yale university, 33
YouTube
   Art of Levitation Unleashed, 37
   Levitating Man Trick Revealed, 38

Made in the USA
Middletown, DE
14 August 2016